THE
AMUSEMENT PARK
OF THE MIND

(ESSAYS ON THOUGHT,
FEELING,
EXPERIENCE)

GREG BACHAR

Books By Greg Bachar

Three-Sided Coin
(Published Works 1990-2003)
2003

Sensual Eye
(The Jack Waste Papers Volume 1: 2004-1991)
2004

Curiosisosity
2013

Dumb Bell & Sticky Foot
(And Other Indulgences)
2013

Beans
(& Other Sundry Items From The General Store)
2013

The Amusement Park Of The Mind
(Essays On Thought, Feeling, Experience)
2013

The Writing Machine
(Writings On Writing: Occasional Ruminations
On An Intangible Legerdemain)
2013

THE AMUSEMENT PARK OF THE MIND

(ESSAYS ON THOUGHT, FEELING, EXPERIENCE)

GREG BACHAR

Rowhouse Press 2013

Acknowledgments

"Remain Awake" and "Oblivion Seeker" were published in *Conduit*. "President Of Planet Earth, Velimir I," "Shock Therapy For The New Millenium," "Keeping The Corpse Alive," "Constant Stranger," "The Light In Darkness," "We're Going To Laugh, Aren't We?," "Conditions Uncertain," "It Wasn't A Dream, It Was A Flood," "Lost And Found In The Lost Domain," "Come Alive!," "Banco," "Bouquet Of Flames," "The Secret Violence Of Henry Miller And How Katy Masuga Made Him That Way," were published in *Rain Taxi Review Of Books*. "What's Going On?," "Science Is The New Art," "The Future," "Love & Heartbreak," "Do You Feel The Joy?" "Twelve Tons Of Chicken" published in *Jack Mackerel Magazine*.

Inquiries:

P.O. Box 23134
Seattle, WA
98102-0434
U.S.A.

ISBN # 0-9719867-4-6

Cover Painting By Matt Dyer

ONE: THOUGHT

TWO: FEELING

THREE: EXPERIENCE

ONE: THOUGHT

VELIMIR KHLEBNIKOV: THE PRESIDENT OF PLANET EARTH, VELIMIR I

"Little things are significant when they mark the start of the future, the way a falling star leaves a strip of fire behind it; they have to be going fast enough to pierce through the present. So far we haven't figured out where they get that speed. But we know a thing is right when it sets the present on fire, like a flint of the future."

Despite the fact that Russian Cubo-Futurist Velimir Khlebnikov only lived a short life of thirty-six years (1885-1922), the volume of work he left behind makes for virtually inexhaustible reading. It is not only the quantity of Khlebnikov's work that may provide the reader with a lifetime of amusement and exhilaration; the scope and nature of his vision of and for the world proves that he was deserving of the titles President Of Planet Earth and The King Of Time. And even though the King Of Time has been dead for almost a hundred years now, his words still seem to have arrived from the future.

"The goal is to create a common written language shared by all the peoples of this third satellite of the Sun, to invent written symbols that can be understood and accepted by our entire star, populated as it is with human beings and lost here in the universe."

Born in the Kalmyk Autonomous Republic in Russia, a region inhabited by Mongolian Buddhist nomads, Khlebnikov grew up to be well-educated in the disciplines of science, nature, folklore, mythology, mathematics, literature, art, history, and languages. By the time he met Mikhail Matiushin, Elena Guro, David Burliuk, Nikolai Kulbin, Vladimir Mayakovsky, Alexei Kruchonykh, and other poets and painters who would become his fellow Futurist cohorts in St. Petersburg and Moscow, Khlebnikov had already begun to fuse these varied subjects in his thinking.

Collaborations with his Futurist peers as they rebelled against the old and musty stodginess of the Symbolists before them helped spark Khlebnikov's literary output.

And while many of the Russian Futurists were talented artists and writers, it is Khlebnikov who, in the end, represents, defines, and keeps Russian Futurism on the literary map today. Khlebnikov is the diamond, so to speak, on the gold band of the Russian Futurist movement.

"I have discovered the fundamental Laws Of Time, and I believe that now it will be easy to predict events as to count to three. If people don't want to learn my art of predicting the future....I shall teach it to horses."

Having published the first two volumes of The Collected Works in 1989, editor Ronald Vroon and Harvard University Press have rounded out the set with Volume III: Selected Poems. When we discover a writer whose work interests us, it is only natural to want to know as much as possible about his or her life.

These three volumes are not only satisfying because of their literary content but because the editor has included a thoughtful and informative biography of Khlebnikov, as well as introductions to the different sections of each volume that provide a context for the different styles and forms that Khlebnikov used to explore his world of ideas.

It is hard not to be interested in this writer who kept his manuscripts in a pillow case under his bed, lectured soldiers in the Red Army on the cycles of time, traveled through Persia in a long beard and tattered clothes as a lecturer/journalist for the Russian government, whose goals for his life's work included the invention of a universal language and alphabet while working mathematically to discover and chart the fundamental algorithms that govern natural and historical events, a discovery that would allow him to do no less than predict the future.

"Those who were inspired by these shadow-book communications were able to go off for a moment, write down their own inspirations, and half an hour later see their messages projected onto those walls in shadow letters by means of the light lens."

Volume I of the series contains Khlebnikov's letters, journals, autobiographical notes, essays on Russia and language, journalistic writings, and his visions of the future, where he predicts or calls for, among other things, the existence of television and global communication, a common system of hieroglyphs for the people of planet Earth, and the creation of a government of Inventors/Explorers to oppose the system of Investors/Exploiters and form an "independent government of time."

Volume II contains Khlebnikov's prose, which he hoped might break the "logical rules of time and space," his plays, and "supersagas," a literary form of his own invention, texts arranged in "canvases" and "planes." "Narrative is architecture composed of words;" he wrote, "an architecture composed of narratives is a 'supersaga.'"

Volume III, as mentioned earlier, contains a generous selection of the six hundred some odd poems that Khlebnikov wrote before his death in 1922. Embellished on the lid of his coffin by Khlebnikov's affectionate friends was a blue planet Earth with the title: "The President Of Planet Earth, Velimir I."

A fitting tribute for a visionary whose literary and aesthetic goal can be summed up as the unification of all the people of Planet Earth.

RENE DAUMAL: REMAIN AWAKE

"You've always been wrong. Like me, like any man, you've let yourself slide down easy, futile slopes."

If the difference between myself and others is the books I read and the ideas I carry around in my head, then I want to read books that will somehow, in some small (or infinite) way, save my life. It usually doesn't take long for me to see that a book has nothing to offer me in the way of aesthetic/philosophical/spiritual "salvation." A page or two, sometimes even a single sentence, is enough to convince me that I have opened a door to a room I do not wish to enter.

On the other hand, sometimes a single page, or a single sentence, shocks me into a startled state of awareness that can only be one thing: recognition. The first page of Rene Daumal's *You've Always Been Wrong* offers the reader a pair of words, a single statement that jolts one into an awareness of the antidote against lethargy, against living a life of clichés and rules dictated to us by others who have never questioned them, who have never questioned themselves.

"What I would like you to try to do with me can be summed up in two words: remain awake."

Every minute of our lives is not, unfortunately, filled with the euphoria and electricity of discovery and creative productivity. Sometimes the workweek is enough to undermine even the slightest act of rebellion.

It is easier to accept and submit to one's fate than it is to rebel, and therein lies the route to the path that allows one's life to crumble into clichés of false contentment. And so there are two possible paths of action, or rather, *re*-action, to follow: sleep, or rebellion.

"But if you have chosen to be, you have set forth on a difficult path which endlessly climbs and demands an unflagging effort. You are awakening; and immediately you have to awaken again. You awaken from your awakening."

Rene Daumal charts out a possible path to a rebellion of the spirit that, if embraced by the individual who feels that his or her life has disassembled into a series of trite or repetitive clichés, will allow him or her to rise above his or her "lot," and to see reality through the liberating lens of the absurd. Once attained, this perspective allows one a new sense of awareness about the way things are, a new sense of

4

humor, and the realization that, in the bigger scheme of things, what we are has less to do with what we do than how we feel about--and what we think about--what we do. If we only define ourselves through our actions in the external, visible world, we will deprive ourselves of the luxury of an internal life of the mind.

"The vision of the intolerable is reason enough to establish for human consciousness the necessity to be transformed."

The writings collected in *You've Always Been Wrong* were written when the author was in his early twenties and still on the road to developing the ideas ultimately sketched out in his unfinished masterpiece *Mount Analogue*, the story of an expedition of mountain climbers and seekers who set out to find an infinite mountain that connects heaven and earth. Active during the height of the Surrealist movement in Paris, Daumal felt their aesthetic was too limiting in its constant need of definitions, declarations, and political alliances. Daumal viewed the awakening of an individual's consciousness as ultimately more beneficial to humanity than Surrealism's alliance with Communism and its revolution of the masses.

"No one can teach you by means of human speech the way to proceed, nor the goal, nor the means, and so I seem to be talking in a void, and yet can men not send out signs of life as a way of helping each other to avoid sleep?"

You've Always Been Wrong charts out the process of awakening to a vision of the absurd and a spiritual revolt against lethargy, against sleep, that accompanies such a rebellion. In his later years (Daumal died of tuberculosis at the age of thirty-six, his life's work fully developed in thought but left unfinished on the page...) Daumal might not have looked so fondly on the essays collected in this volume, as they attempt to use language to describe states of consciousness that are nearly impossible to describe in words. But the fact that Daumal's words so vividly lead one as far as one can go before reaching the edge and outer limits of one's thinking about the world, the abstract nature of definitions, and of the world itself, allows this book, in conjunction with the rest of Daumal's writing, to act as a valuable map for those who might like to follow in his footsteps and continue the journey he himself began as the continuation of a journey years ago.

"I say that the first step is to awaken absolutely so as to deserve to sleep like a rock, in a sleep transmuted into a universal consciousness."

ANDRE BRETON:
KEEPING THE CORPSE ALIVE

The day I began reading *Revolution Of The Mind*, Mark Polizzotti's biography of Andre Breton, a story in the newspaper caught my eye. "Corpse Did Not Decompose In Three Years: Police Suspect Dry Ice," the headline read.

Breton, the founding father and main proponent of Surrealism, might have appreciated the story of a grieving Hong Kong widow who kept her dead husband's body on ice, hoping that he would somehow come back to life. Her children, who delivered the dry ice each day, finally reported her to the authorities, despite her threat to kill herself if they told anyone.

This story led me to muse for a while on the role of the biographer who, like the grieving widow, hopes not only to preserve the deceased in question, but to bring him or her back to life using only words, anecdotal material, and the memories of those who knew the subject during their time on Earth—no dry ice allowed.

In this respect, *Revolution Of The Mind* succeeds on many levels. While covering what must have been every major event of Breton's seventy years, it also paints a vivid portrait of the times in which this visionary and ambitious thinker lived and wrote.

Not merely satisfied, though, to place the man in the context of his time, Polizzotti has also written a definitive introduction, overview, and history of the Surrealist movement from its playful beginnings to the death of its leader forty years later, by which time it had cast a worldwide spell in the art and literary world.

Although Mr. Polizzotti mentions nearly every one of the principals involved in the movement as it evolved and transformed over the years, it is obvious by the end of the book that without Breton's playing the role of hub or anchor to the galaxy of literary and artistic stars that gathered around him, the constellation of Surrealism would not exist.

A universe of mad and marvelous moments, *Revolution Of The Mind* brings to life the ups and downs, successes and failures, loves and desires of one of the twentieth century's truly mad geniuses.

JACQUES VACHE:
WE'RE GOING TO LAUGH, AREN'T WE?

Writers who die young and full of promise leave behind a wake upon which others surf until that wake fades to ripples and disappears. Some who make early exits leave larger wakes than others. So it is with Andre Breton's friend and fellow provocateur Jacques Vache, who died of an opium overdose in 1919 at the age of twenty-three.

Echoes of Vache's ideas reverberate throughout the founding father of Surrealism's work; Breton himself wrote, "It is to Jacques Vache that I owe the most." He was haunted by Vache's life and death and surfed the wake he left behind for the duration of his own much longer life, periodically explaining and mythologizing his dead friend.

And so it is with Franklin Rosemont's *Jacques Vache And The Roots Of Surrealism*, a nearly 400-page book devoted to the study of a man whose total creative output was a smattering of sketches and sixteen pages of letters and short prose pieces scribbled while stationed at the French front in World

War I. How can this be? A simple word problem provides one possible answer: Jacques Vache was to _____ as Neal Cassady was to _____.

If you guessed "Surrealism" and "the Beat Movement," you are correct, but it might be more accurate to say that Vache was to Andre Breton as Neal Cassady was to Jack Kerouac: Man Muse.

And yet "this is not a biography," Rosemont writes; "the interruptions, distractions and gaps in Vache's hectic and even incoherent life preclude a 'formal' and/or chronological 'life.' Like the book's subject, whose many virtues included a strong disdain for 'following orders,' the book itself likewise follows no order."

And so the book wanders from chapter to chapter like rooms in a house built out of bricks made out of Jacques Vache. In one room, the writer's life and death occupies a corner; in another reside World War I and the daily life of soldiers; in yet another dandyism is defined and the fact that Vache was one of the three greatest dandies of his time is pondered. Over by the window: the books and films Vache read and viewed and the books and films he *might* have read and viewed. Other chapters include explorations of Alfred Jarry and Pataphysics, anarchism, laughter, Vache's influence on Surrealism, and Vache's drawings and war Letters.

It seems a bit odd that Vache's writing is located at the end of the book; by the time one finally reaches this room, it is easy to be let down by his short stack of letters, reviews, and prose pieces. On the other hand, Rosemont has prepared the reader well for this encounter, so the reader will want to decide for themselves how to progress: Vache first, Vache last, or a mix of both.

Vache is best known as the inventor of *umor*, which Andre Breton later called *black humor*. When asked by Breton to define *umor*, Vache wrote: "I believe it is a sensation—I was going to say a SENSE—also—of the theatrical (and joyless) uselessness of everything. When one knows." Vache's definition doesn't need further explication;

one either gets it or they don't. In this regard, black humor remains the same today.

Rosemont makes a valid point, though, when he expands on Vache's definition by writing "the umorist—inspired, illuminating, and attracted to all that is truly alive—deploys scandal to *expand* consciousness, thereby participating in the *becoming of freedom.*"

A key idea here is that it is the responsibility of the *living* to expand on the ideas of those who have passed before, and in this regard Rosemont's book succeeds splendidly.

Jacques Vache's legacy is the idea that liberation from the mundane can be achieved through the power of humor and absurdity. It is an unfinished legacy without end, one that reminds the reader how necessary it is that every generation needs to have such individuals who push, prod and ask, like Vache:

"What next? We're going to laugh, aren't we?"

THE SECRET VIOLENCE
OF HENRY MILLER AND HOW
KATY MASUGA MADE HIM THAT WAY

In his essay "Writers Lost In The Distance," Roberto Bolaño describes "remembering the writers who were important to us in our youth and who today have fallen into a kind of oblivion . . . We thought, of course, of Henry Miller." Katy Masuga attempts to rescue Miller from oblivion with her critical studies *The Secret Violence Of Henry Miller* and *Henry Miller And How He Got That Way*.

One of Masuga's fundamental points in *The Secret Violence* is that "writing can only ever grapple at a truth that is the manifestation of a collection of subjective experiences, or, rather, the expression of subjective experiences, which are experiences that become forced and into a collection that becomes the book . . . Order is not made through language," she adds, "as nothing is actually made through language in a concrete and final sense."

Miller addresses this notion in a passage from *Tropic Of Capricorn*: "I must have the ability and the patience to formulate what is not contained in the language of our time, for what is now intelligible is meaningless. My eyes are useless, for they render back only the image of the known."

Masuga, looking through the lens of Maurice Blanchot, responds: "if writing is defining what is unknown . . . it must always leave the unknown to be unknown, even though its purpose is the attempt to uncover and to disclose that unknown."

Why, then, should one read these books that attempt to make "known" various "unknown" aspects of Miller's writing? Masuga might refer the reader to an earlier passage in the book where she explores Miller's idea that "this was the business of authorship, as I then conceived it. Make mud puddles, if necessary, but see to it that they reflect the galactic varnish." In response to Miller and addressing the reader, she writes:

> The galaxy is the unknown world as we project it before ourselves, despite the fact that its varnish is evidence of a deliberate finishing on a stupendous scale. We do not see its transparency, however, but the grandeur of the galaxy only as reflected in the mud puddles we make, and yet we mystify it through that reflected presence. We feel incapable of ever seeing the surface of the galaxy: how it shines, how it is already finished (by us). We come to imagine it as impenetrable, when in fact it is created—and subsequently easily accessible—through the activity of mud puddle-making: through the intellect, which is language and, hence, is the act of writing. Language, particularly writing itself, is the tool we create for ourselves as intellectualizing beings to understand the mysteries that our own intellectualizing created.

Masuga makes such heady stuff interesting through extensive sampling of examples and sources to create thick mash-up layers of theory, language, influence, and intertextuality that form the analytical basis for both volumes. A brief section of *Henry Miller And How He Got That Way* serves as an excellent example of her technique.

In response to Miller's statement that, "long before I read Wittgenstein's *Tractatus Logico-Philosophicus* I was composing music to it, in the key of sassafras," Masuga brings Proust, Cezanne, Bosch, Chagall, Matisse, Baudelaire, Rimbaud, Carroll, Wittgenstein, synesthesia, word play, and language games into the proceedings to illustrate that Miller, "as usual, is engaging in multiple forms of intertextuality" and "literary correspondence that can transcend space and time" between himself and his ancestral authors.

Masuga explores four forms of intertextuality in *Henry Miller And How He Got That Way*: "Miller's direct allusions to his influences;" "styles that are unconsciously borrowed;" "reverse influence . . . the manner in which the manifestation of the writer of influence in Miller's work has perhaps affected a new reception of that figure of influence in subsequent criticism;" and "with Miller presenting the writer of influence as a figure in the text, occasionally even as a character." Masuga selects Miller's ancestral authors Walt Whitman, Fyodor Dostoyevsky, Lewis Carroll, Arthur Rimbaud, Marcel Proust, and D.H. Lawrence as the central figures for the book's explorations of these four forms.

The Secret Violence Of Henry Miller is the more spaciously-written and linear book of the two, though not as much referential fun. Masuga's goal here is to "suggest a new way of reading Miller that is alert to the aggressively writerly and self-conscious form of his work." To accomplish this, she's divided the book into chapters that explore categorization of Miller's work by others, a study by Deleuze and Guattani on "minor literature," metaphor, Miller's descriptions of objects and places, his use of motion, time, and space, and the presence of visual and literary arts in Miller's work.

Both books summon a long list of supporting characters. Blanchot, Deleuze, Guattari, Derrida, Bataille, and Barthes get star billing with additional appearances by an epic multitude of others, a very short list of whom includes the likes of Harold Bloom, Marcel Duchamp, James Joyce, Anais Nin, Francois Villon, Samuel Beckett, Borges, Coleridge, Byron, Nietzsche, and Charlie Chaplin.

Where some of Miller's ideas and attitudes seem handcuffed to the times in which he lived, Masuga aims toward the future of critical theory. And while she succeeds in achieving her goals for both books, it's hard to see these efforts sparking a Henry Miller renaissance. It's more likely that readers will want to read more Masuga, but who knows? As Roberto Bolaño points out:

> The explanation for the ebb of writers . . . is very simple. Just as love moves according to a mechanism like the sea's, as the Nicaraguan poet Martinez Rivas puts it, so too do writers move, and one day they appear and then they disappear and then maybe they disappear again. And if they don't, it really doesn't matter so much, because in some secret way, they're us now.

THOUGHTS ABOUT DWELLING

Heidegger's "Building Dwelling Thinking" is a text that can be applied to many different topics besides simply "dwelling." The piece is more an exercise in thought and language than a specific analysis of the difference between building and dwelling or the connection between them.

It is clear that "not every building is a dwelling." Heidegger could have been writing about many things with this statement, but textual contexts raised by the reading of a written work come to mind. Some texts bend to interpretation while others break.

Some texts suggest, lead to, or imply "meaning" just as "dwelling" implies more than merely shelter, while other texts imply nothing or do not give way to interpretation, just as buildings that are not dwellings do not support "dwelling."

There are texts that are "built" to (seemingly) accommodate interpretation—The Bible, Joyce's *Ulysses*, while other texts such as advertisements, packaging labels and street signs serve only utilitarian functions.

It is as if Heidegger has implied, without specifically saying it, that some texts support thought and inspire language through discussion while others just hang in the air; that some texts are built to dwell in, while others are built just to be built.

The question that this raises has to do with the veracity of a "thing" that is brought into the world through thought. Heidegger gathers and assembles this "essay thing" of his and calls it "Building Dwelling Thinking." To steal a phrase from Heidegger, the essay "gathers to itself in its own way earth and sky, divinities and mortals."

When Heidegger talks about the bridge, he says that if it is a true bridge, it does not become a symbol after becoming a bridge, but is a thing that gathers the fourfold. But a bridge does begin as a symbol, as an idea in someone's head, before it is realized as a bridge-thing in the concrete world of building materials. And once it is a bridge, it can be a symbol *and* a bridge, just as the Berlin Wall was a wall marking a border and also a symbol of oppression (and finally a symbol of the dismantling of oppression). Does the wall gather the fourfold only in its material realization, or is the idea of the wall enough to accomplish this?

There are things that have never been assigned symbolic meanings, such as an ice cream scoop or a cheese grater. They are simple utilitarian things that began as thoughts in their makers' minds. If symbolic meaning had somehow descended on these two items, though, they would then become the equivalent of dwellings, in which there is meaning and value. But since the thought behind these things was purely utilitarian, and since they are things that could only be used as symbols of oppression in a strangely warped world, they remain as things.

A text, then, is like a building. It is either meant for building or for dwelling in the reader's mind. Over time, a given text that might have been overlooked earlier may be assigned meaning and gain the value of a dwelling. Or that text might continue to be ignored and remain a simple thing. It seems, then, that a text works the same way as a building. It begins as an idea in the mind that, when realized, gathers the fourfold Heidegger speaks of. If a text is realized as a thing and presented to the reading world, its readers determine if it is a "dwelling text" or if it is only a text-thing, a hollow shell uninhabitable by the mind seeking the shelter of elevation and enlightenment.

When Heidegger asks the following question in the last paragraph of "Building Dwelling Thinking," his answer seems to be an idea that can be applied to more than a simple examination of dwellings. He asks, "how else can mortals answer this summons than by trying on their part, on their own, to bring dwellings to the fullness of its nature," to which he answers, "this they accomplish when they build out of dwelling, and think for the sake of dwelling."

Heidegger's answer, to a writer, seems to be an inspiration to create texts that are full of meaning and possibility that reflect the gathering of the fourfold, texts that are alive with the dwelling life of the writer, lives that are rich with the density of dwelling, and language that furthers itself and is not only noise.

DWELLING BY THE COURSE
OF THOUGHT HERE ATTEMPTED

Heidegger touches upon the mysterious and silent core of creativity when he encompasses the fourfold in his "essay-thing" "Building Dwelling Thinking." Heidegger writes in almost allegorical terms, so that his metaphors ("dwelling," "bridges," "building") easily bend to interpretation that can be applied to many subjects. But the "THING" at the center of the "thing" appears in the first paragraph of the work: "not every building is a dwelling."

Heidegger has written a basic treatise on Art that encompassed more than just the fourfold, but the origin of the fourfold from which Art acts as a bridge between banks of the imagination, between the creator and those who experience the creator's work, either through interpretation and analysis or for simple aesthetic enjoyment.

Heidegger's demand is that building and dwelling be worth something: "Enough will have been gained if dwelling and building have become worthy of questioning and thus have remained worthy of thought." Can the creator of a work of art decide whether something he or she creates will become worthy of questioning or that it will remain worthy of thought? This is where Heidegger's text is divided. There is the issue of creation and the issue of interpretation. Is there a meeting point between the two? Does one encompass the other, as dwelling encompasses the fourfold? Heidegger's metaphor of the bridge seems to answer these questions.

He writes, "[The bridge] does not just connect banks that are already there. The banks emerge as banks only as the bridge crosses the stream." One can visualize the metaphor of the bridge to stand for a poem. A poem, then, is a bridge between two banks: the bank of the creator/poet, and the bank of the interpreter/reader. Neither "bank" exists until the "bridge" between them exists. One is dependent on the other. The writer creates it, brings it to life, but it does not truly exist without the reader to complete the bridge.

Paul Celan, in a speech he gave after receiving the Georg Buchner Prize in 1960, said, "The poem is lonely. It is lonely and en route. Its author stays with it. Does this very fact not place the poem already here, at its inception, in the encounter, in the mystery of encounter? The poem intends another, needs this other, and needs an opposite. It goes toward it, bespeaks it." The poem is the dwelling, but it needs to be dwelled in to be a bridge between banks.

"The bridge is a location," Heidegger writes. "As such a thing, it allows a space into which earth and heaven, divinities and mortals are admitted." This space is occupied by the poem, which creates and/or inspires its own boundaries and rules for being read.

"A boundary is not that at which something stops," he states, "but, as the Greeks recognized, the boundary is that from which something begins its presencing." The poem, once it has bridged its two banks, begins to exist as its own "space." The reader can visit and occupy this space on the page in a book.

The poem is a location that has the potential to encompass the fourfold. "Building puts up locations that make space and a site for the fourfold. The poem is a built thing, just like Heidegger's essay, just like this essay. The poem is built to encompass the fourfold. It is made as something to "appear" to those who have not seen it before to encompass the fourfold, and to induce revelation and/or recognition. The poet lets his or her poem appear. It then exists as a dwelling for our otherwise voiceless thoughts and feelings, the sensations that encompass the fourfold. It is specially constructed to fulfill the encompassing of the fourfold.

Heidegger asks that the poet be aware of this and that he think and create to dwell, because, "Only if we are capable of dwelling, only then can we build." The poem, then, is a group of words that is more than just a group of words—it is a dwelling in which one is able to exist with the fourfold.

The poet bridges the gap between what readers feel by providing them with words to describe those feelings. Language bridges the silent banks with understanding.

WAITING FOR GODOT AT MONTPARNASSE

I imagine a performance of Samuel Beckett's *Waiting For Godot* taking place in the Montparnasse cemetery in Paris where the author has been laid to rest. What better place to put on the play than in a cemetery? What better grave to use as center stage than Beckett's?

This performance of Beckett's classic play probably would have amused the author as much as it did the excited Paris crowd who came to pay tribute to the deceased writer. It was not at all a somber rendering of *Waiting For Godot*, even with the eerie backdrop and many audience members taking in the play from their graves. Instead, the play's comedic elements once again served to underscore the plight of Vladimir and Estragon as they wait for Godot to appear, as if Beckett was saying that man's greatest trait is his ability to laugh in the face of death.

The audience was escorted in a roundabout way to Beckett's grave. Groups of fifty at a time were led from the main gate by a stooped figure dressed in rags and laden with heavy baggage, who later played Lucky during the performance. A taller man, thin-faced with a pipe in mouth, advised the groups to remain silent until seated next to the stage, and sent Lucky off with audience members in tow with a sharp crack of his leather whip. The group was led slowly past Sartre's grave, then Baudelaire's, before being pulled through a zigzag maze of narrow alleys between gravestones so that, once they had arrived at their seats, each group was made to feel alienated from the world of the living they had left behind at the cemetery's gates.

Once seated around Beckett's grave, upon which a lone tree has been planted in a shallow mound of fresh earth, the audience was made to wait for the play to begin just long enough for some to become restless, some to fidget and sigh, and some to suggest to their companions that they leave, while the majority resigned themselves to the wait and immersed themselves in idle chatter to pass the time. Starting time was listed as eight o'clock, but the play didn't begin until

17

nine-thirty. One imagines this was a ploy on the part of the director that forced the audience to react to their period of waiting just as Estragon and Vladimir react to theirs, though for all we know there may have simply been technical difficulties that delayed the start of the performance.

An expansive white scrim was hung behind Beckett's gravestone. A single bare tree was erected atop the stone, planted in a low mound of fresh earth. The scrim emphasized the blank, empty space surrounding the characters as they wait for Godot. Like ink marks on an otherwise empty page, Vladimir and Estragon appeared against the scrim as if sketched into the scene. They appeared small in relation to the emptiness that surrounded and loomed above them.

The physical gestures in the play used against the largeness of the empty scrim served as a kind of mime play within the play. Not only do Vladimir and Estragon talk to pass their time, they move and hit each other, panic and run around when they think a possible attack is coming from a group of unseen individuals, and attempt to dance, though in slapstick fashion. When the audience laughed, they fulfilled one of the play's themes, that man will find ways to laugh and act and pass the time, however futile, while waiting for whatever Godot represents in their individual lives.

The use of the cemetery as setting for the play was appropriate as a counter to much of Beckett's language. Every underscored silence between exchanges of dialogue allowed the audience to feel the silence in the act of waiting, but also the sounds of the graveyard at night.

Midway through the play, Vladimir and Estragon ask themselves why they are talking to one another. They realize it is a way for them to pass the time, "so we don't hear....all the dead voices...they make a noise like wings....like leaves....they murmur....they rustle." Such is the atmosphere of the Montparnasse Cemetery, a virtual city of the dead where one's stroll, even on a sunny day, is injected with the overwhelming presence of wandering souls.

Staging *Waiting For Godot* in the cemetery underscored the fact that, although Vladimir and Estragon are waiting for some manifestation of the elusive Godot to appear, their talk and actions suggest that their lives are spent trying to distract themselves from the eventual death that awaits them and that, in this production, surrounds them as well as us, the audience, also sitting in wait.

DWELLING FOR GODOT
ON MONKEY MOUNTAIN

Martin Heidegger describes the existence of a thing in the world by using a metaphor of a bridge between banks in his essay "Building Dwelling Thinking." He explains that the bridge is a location that presents possibilities to both banks that it touches. The banks themselves only begin to exist after the bridge has been built when the two sides have been touched. Each bank, following the existence of the bridge, is presented with the possibility of "the other side." Those on one bank may cross to the other, and vice versa. This crossing over encompasses what Heidegger terms "the fourfold," "a space into which earth and heaven, divinities and mortals are admitted." The fourfold describes a point at which four lines cross to form a whole.

First, the earth, "the serving bearer, blossoming and fruiting, spreading out in rock and water, rising up into plant and animal." This is the base from which all life, all creative endeavors, has emerged. Second is the sky, the heavens, "the wandering glitter of the stars, the year's seasons and their changes, the light and dusk of day, the gloom and glow of night, the clemency and inclemency of the weather, the drifting clouds and blue depth of the ether." The sky, in metaphorical terms, is the blank screen that the artist projects his ideas against. While pondering the empty spaces, he discovers a thing with which to fill the space. Third are the divinities, "the beckoning messengers of the godhead. Out of the holy sway of the godhead, the god appears in his presence or withdraws into his concealment." The artist, in his search for something in the heavens, discovers relics left behind by the gods—ideas and truths. Fourth in the fourfold are the mortals, "the human beings. They are called mortals because they can die. To die means to be capable of death *as* death. Only man dies, and indeed continually, as long as he remains on earth, under the sky, before the divinities." The artist is mortal and, while dying, lives his life in a state of discovery and creation. He builds things that previously did not exist. Once they do exist, these things act as bridges between the banks of incomprehension to stimulate understanding.

According to Heidegger, it is through the building of things that Man dwells on the earth. He differentiates between mere building, the utilitarian production of things for purely utilitarian purposes, and dwelling, which "preserves the fourfold by bringing the presencing of the fourfold into things." When a thing is built with dwelling in mind, it will enable the mortal to stimulate thought and the creation of new ideas. When Man encompasses the fourfold with something that he has created for his mind to dwell in, he not only affirms his existence, but also confirms the fact that he is one part of a whole that connects the earth with the sky with the divine. In creating things such as plays, he dwells as part of something greater than himself. In creating things that stimulate the mind to react through thought, Man(kind) preserves his whole self, bringing together the utilitarian self with the aesthetic self who enjoys the pleasures of the creation of a work of art.

Heidegger's essay suggests the potency of the building materials used to create "dwellings" lies in the fact that "it is language that tells us about the nature of a thing." Words are used to build things that possess or inspire meaning, thought and interpretation and with language, bridges are created, boundaries broken. "A boundary is not that at which something stops but, as the Greeks recognized, the boundary is that from which something begins its presencing." To break a boundary, Heidegger suggests, is to open up the presence of possibility and expand thought, thus increasing the space of potential to limitless size. A play, then, which is a thing created with language, is a bridge between banks, while also a broken/expanded boundary. Its goal is a change in the consciousness of its audience that will result in an expansion of thought, or a change that will inspire action.

The play, while a thing of words, is also a thing of action. The play, with its connection of audience, stage and author, also serves to encompass Heidegger's fourfold, thus fulfilling the need to build out of dwelling and thought rather than just utility. Derek Walcott's introductory essay to *Dream On Monkey Mountain*, "What The Twilight Says: An Overture," contains a Heideggerian undercurrent of ideas that parallel some aspects of "Building Dwelling Thinking." As examples of texts that encompass the fourfold, I saw *Dream On Monkey Mountain* and *Waiting For Godot* as two plays which fulfilled Heidegger's demand that a "building," a work of art, "be worthy of questioning and thus have remained worthy of thought." Each play, as text, is an example of thought/action-provoking language. Each play encompasses the fourfold, connecting the viewer with the different aspects of his existence: the earth, the sky, the divine, and himself.

Walcott initiates his introductory essay with a meditation on the sky and the destitute, when "deprivation is made lyrical, and twilight, with the patience of alchemy, almost transmutes despair into virtue." He goes on to examine, in metaphorical terms, how he desired to find a language to put into words this despair that he observed, that he, the writer, "proffered silently the charity of a language which they could not speak." This language, though, when Walcott was still searching for his "true" language, was "reflective and mannered, as far above its subjects as that sun which would never set until its twilight became a metaphor for the withdrawal of Empire and the beginning of our doubt." With this in mind, Walcott's role became one of "builder" in search of the proper building materials—the right words. He recognizes the fact that he and the actor who will act out the writer's words, to get at the root of the soul of a liberated people, to create a new language of theatre, must "record the anguish of the race. To do this, they must return through a darkness whose terminus is amnesia. The darkness that yawns before them is terrifying. It is the journey back from man to ape."

Heidegger expresses a similar notion. He suggests that man must constantly re-learn how to dwell, "that mortals ever search anew for the nature of dwelling, that they must ever learn to dwell." He speaks of mankind's inherent homelessness and the fact that there is a constant process of discovering how to build, live, dwell and survive in the midst of that homelessness. In textual terms, silence and incomprehension are equated with homelessness. Once man can find the words to describe and explore his state of homelessness, or primitive wordlessness, he is no longer as lost a being as his mute primal self.

Walcott's journey is one through words as he attempts to create and recreate a liberated language, somehow free of its Colonial connotations, while also placing his work in the context of the world as a whole. It is a journey with the goal of creating a long-term linguistic dwelling to be rooted in theatre, "in the faith that one was creating not merely a play, but a theatre, and not merely a theatre, but its environment." The goal is not just theatre, but a language of theatre, not just words, but words worthy of thought, words to liberate the liberated body's mind: "What would deliver him from servitude," Walcott writes, "was the forging of a language that went beyond mimicry, a dialect which had the force of revelation as it invented names for things, one which finally settled on its own mode of inflection, and which began to create an oral culture of chants, folk-songs and fables; this, not merely the debt of history was his proper claim to the New World."

Dream On Monkey Mountain is about this search for new words and a way of words to forge new ways of the world. The fact that it is a dream underscores the encompassing of the divine by the dreamer's mind. The dream is seen as something above man's consciousness, since it comes when he sleeps, and is sent as a message from the godhead, the psyche. Makak has the dream of the white lady, a voice of the godhead, and he descends from his mountain with the power that he alone possesses. He wants to lead the people back to Africa. In a sense, he wants to return them to where the old language waits for them, but to get back to this rootedness, there must first be a transformation during which a new language is forged, ultimately resulting in self-realization. Makak explains where the power for such a transformation must come: "The mind, the mind. Now, come with me, the mind can bring the dead to life, it can go back, back, back, deep into time." Makak climbs down from Monkey Mountain to speak the words that, until that moment, had been only thoughts inside his head. He descends from the mountain into the silence of the incomprehension of the mute masses. He descends to exercise his power. He descends to grant language to a voiceless, impoverished nation.

Makak, in this respect, parallels the writer who possesses the words with which transformation can be made possible. He is educated, he knows how to use the words, but he must first learn how to speak a language that the people without education, without the use of language, will be able to understand and utilize as their own. This is what the creation of Walcott's personal theatre encompassed. The fact that, after twenty years of working towards this end, Walcott has still not seen his ideals fulfilled underscores Heidegger's point that expression is an ongoing affair. "When twenty years ago we imagined cities devoted neither to power nor to money but to art," Walcott writes, "one had the true vision." Is Makak's dream a failure, then, because it fails to come true in the play's "real" world? No, because his dream represents the possibility of action, the potential of words to create new worlds. Makak's poetry is the poetry of possibility. It raises the issue of his peoples' misery and in doing so substitutes this potential for rootedness where before there had only been rootlessness.

Samuel Beckett's "dwelling" of words in *Waiting For Godot* encompasses Heidegger's fourfold in an entirely different way. It accepts mankind's homelessness as well as the fact of his mute wordlessness. While waiting for the godhead to appear, Vladimir and Estragon generate a lot of noise, but don't say much. This is why so much of *Waiting For Godot* is funny, even though Vladimir and Estragon are sad figures. They represent the failure of individuals to fill their existence with the building of dwellings because they accept the godhead's absence at face value. In Beckett's play, the godhead, Godot, fails to appear to Vladimir and Estragon. "In the very depth of misfortune they wait for the weal that has been withdrawn," Heidegger writes. They fill their time with idle chatter, trivial repetitions and senseless games. They represent the opposite of dwelling.

It is Beckett's language, then, not Vladimir and Estragon, that encompasses the fourfold, inspires an awareness of the earth, the sky, the divine and mortality. The observer of Beckett's play senses the absence of the godhead, the bareness of the earth (the empty stage), the misery of waiting for something that will never appear, and realizes that, in the face of this endless misery, he or she must build a dwelling and encompass the fourfold for themselves.

Walcott's dream world is similar, but different. *Dream On Monkey Mountain* raises the possibility and potential of a language used to create permanent dwellings for man's liberated identity (while also recognizing the potential for abuse of this power once realized). At the end of the play, the dreamer wakes up and returns to where he came from, to continue the daily work. The play, then, is one possibility among many; the work must continue to evolve. In Beckett's world, the futility of inaction, of paralysis, is emphasized. If we say nothing, if we do not attempt to dwell, to build things worthy of thought, there is no godhead figure that will descend to fill our time for us. There is no use waiting. Like Walcott and Beckett, the individual must find his or her own language, and use it to build his or her own bridge of comprehension.

OUTLAWS AND OUTLAWRY:
THE PENAL CODE OF ICELANDIC SAGAS

"The more underhanded the deed, the greater the punishment..." 1

The people who first settled in Iceland were rather unique for colonists looking for a better place to live. They didn't just take their families and belongings to their new home, claim some land, and begin a new life. Instead, the early Icelanders recognized the need for a set of laws to maintain order on what was to begin with, a limited area of land.

First, they set a limit on the number of settlers allowed into Iceland, then they set up their own government, their own constitution, their own legislative body, and their own set of laws. The Icelanders, with the laws, also recognized the need to maintain order in Iceland by limiting violent acts, and a penal code was instituted as well.

The early laws of Iceland were not such that they were meant to alienate the people from their own legislative system. Rather, the laws were meant for all parties involved to settle disputes, arbitrations, and any problems between landowners.

In conjunction with the laws, there were several courses of action open to the Icelander when a dispute had come up. He might settle the matter himself by taking the law into his own hands. 2 He might settle the matter directly with the other person or group of people involved, through arbitration. 3 Or, the case could be brought to court and settled there. 4

At the courts, punishments were handed out according to the magnitude of the crime. Lesser crimes usually resulted in fines, while for greater crimes outlawry was the most common form of punishment. So, three kinds of punishment made up Iceland's early penal code: the handing out of fines, lesser outlawry, full outlawry, or any combination of the three, as arbitrated in each individual case. 5

Iceland's early penal code and system of punishments is essentially based on the fact that troublemakers were to be removed from where they were creating a problem (through outlawry), either temporarily, so that the tensions between feuding parties could be erased with the passage of time, or permanently, to insure that those involved never disrupt the natural order in Iceland again. 6

Either way, the basis of early Icelandic law can be defined in the following quote from an introduction to *Gragas*, the laws, by Dennis, Foote, and Perkins: "All free people enjoyed the same legal status but their immunity or right to legal redress might be diminished or lost by their own act." 7

In other words, the laws that were open for all Icelanders to use for their own good would be closed to them if they disrupted others' rights to the laws. The laws reflect an attitude that it was a great privilege to live in Iceland and that harming the land or its people would lead to the loss of this privilege.

Wrongdoers were outlawed and removed from Iceland, not contained in prisons. The source of the problem was eliminated. It is obvious that a great importance was placed on freedom in early Iceland, and perhaps outlawry as a form of punishment reflects this. To be banished, one has lost his homeland but is still a free man, able to go where he wants to go (although he may have a problem with this as a full outlaw), rather than being boxed in, a prisoner in one's own land.

Court cases were heard each year at the Althing, with minor cases dealing with minor crimes being handled at the spring or quarter assemblies. 8 Judges were appointed the day before the opening of the Althing, on a Friday, and the courts began two days later. 9 Testimony from witnesses was heard, and the courts decided if the party involved was guilty or not guilty. 10 Sentences, as stated before, consisted of fines, lesser outlawry, full outlawry, or a combination of the three.

The Icelandic term for a lesser outlaw is *fjorbaugsmadr*. To be a *fjorbaugsmadr* meant that the person was either banished from one district, or *heradssekr*, for a period of time, or he had to leave Iceland for three years. 11 In this case, the outlaw was *sekr um allt land*, not allowed to be in Iceland. 12 Lesser outlawries were always given in conjunction with a fine, or *fjorbaugr*. The *fjorbaugr* was the fine necessary for a lesser outlaw to pay to avoid becoming a full outlaw. If he was unable to pay this fine, the guilty man became a full outlaw, or *skogarmadr*. 13

The word *fjorbaugr* means, in terms of the law, "life-ring," and a lesser outlaw was called a "life-ring man," apparently because rings of silver were used in Iceland rather than solid bars or coins, with the amount of silver required for the payment of a fine being cut off from the ring. 14

If a convict was outlawed from one district or area, he was free to live in other parts of Iceland. But if he was to leave Iceland, he had to meet certain conditions and requirements to avoid becoming a full outlaw, or *skogarmadr*.

The lesser outlaw, or *fjorbaugsmadr*, was given three years to find a ship out of Iceland. He was required to ask three ship owners a year to take him out of Iceland, and those ship owners who refused were fined three marks of silver. 15

If the life-ring man, or *fjorbaugsmadr*, did not find a way out of Iceland in three years, he would be made a full outlaw and would lose his *heilgar*, that is, protection by the law of Iceland.

To be *heilgar* means that the *fjorbaugsmadr* was allowed three residencies that could be no more than a day's journey apart. 16 He could travel between these only once a month, on the road, or an arrow's shot or spear's throw to the side of the road. If he fulfilled all these requirements, the lesser outlaw was still protected by the laws of Iceland, and in the three years he had to stay out of Iceland after finding passage, he was *heilgar* as well, wherever he went. 17

If a *fjorbaugsmadr* committed another crime with a sentence of outlawry, if he did not satisfy the terms of his outlawry, and if he did not find a way out of Iceland, he was automatically made a full outlaw. However, if he did satisfy all terms of being *fjorbaugsmadr*, he could return to Iceland in three years and continue his life there.

Full outlawry, or *fullsekta*, was the severest form of punishment in Icelandic law. The full outlaw, or *skogarmadr*, meant that a man no longer had any legal rights and could be killed by anyone without having to answer to the law. Besides losing his legal rights, the *skogarmadr* could not be given aid or passage out of the country, and anyone who did so would also be subject to penalty by the law. 18

As Dennis, Foote, and Perkins state in their introduction to their translation of *Gragas*, "Full outlawry meant loss of all goods through a confiscation court, loss of all status, and denial of all assistance—virtually a death penalty." 19 Additionally, all of the *skogarmadr's* social connections to Iceland were dissolved, everything from marriage, kinship, right of inheritance, property, and even his right to a Christian burial. 20 In essence, full outlawry demoted the guilty party down to the level of a non-person; the *skogarmadr* might as well have never been born.

Although full outlawry meant almost definite death, there was no police force in Iceland to carry out the punishment, so in some cases, convicts were able to survive using their wits and strength for years following their sentence of outlawry. 21 If the outlaw was able to stay alive for twenty years he became a free man again. Only one man came close to accomplishing this feat, Grettir "The Strong" Asmundsson, who lived through his outlawry for nineteen years until he was finally brought down. 22

Both lesser and full outlawry led to the confiscation of property by a confiscation court fourteen days after the end of a particular court session, so perhaps a word should be mentioned about this.

The court of confiscation, or *feransdomr*, consisted of twelve judges who were chosen by the prosecutor's *godi*, chieftain, of the area in which the prosecutor lived. 23 These judges paid off the outlaw's creditors, gave a cow or an ox to the *godi*, with half of the remaining property going to the prosecutor, the other half given to the men of the quarter in which the outlaw, or *utlagi*, lived. 24

In *Hoensa-Thoris Saga*, both lesser and full outlawry are passed down as sentences on the guilty parties who were involved in the burning death of Blund-Ketill. At the Althing, Arngrimigodi and others involved in the plot to kill Blund-Ketill are pronounced full outlaws, and Thorvald Oddsson is made a lesser outlaw and banished for three years:

"They now set to debating these same cases, and the end of it was that Arngrim the Priest should be made a full outlaw, and all those who were present at the burning, except for Thorvald Oddson. He must go abroad for three years and then be free to come back." 25

In *Njal's Saga*, the process of sentencing which leads to the lesser outlawry of Gunnar and his brother Kolskegg is referred to. Gunnar had killed Thorgeirr Otkelsson, hence killing twice in the same family:

"Many other chieftains supported this call for a settlement, and eventually it was agreed that twelve men should arbitrate. Both parties came forward and shook hands on this agreement. The arbitration was made and the amount of compensation determined. The entire sum was to be paid up at once at the Althing. Furthermore, Gunnar and Kolskegg were to leave the country for three years..." 26

Both a fine and a sentence of lesser outlawry are passed down which, for Gunnar, is later upped to full outlawry when he refuses to leave the country. *Gisli Saga* is the story of Gisli, who is outlawed early on, with the rest of the story dealing with his life while outlawed, all the way to his death. Gisli was able to live as an outlaw for six years before he was brought down.

He spends his three years as a lesser outlaw traveling throughout Iceland looking for support from chieftains to oppose his outlawry, but he finds none and at the end of the three years is made a full outlaw, subject to the instant loss of all rights and instant death by anyone who chose to kill him:

"It is told that Gisli was three years in Geirthjot's fjord, but now and again with Thorkel Eiriksson, and the next three years he goes all about Iceland and visits the chieftains and asks for their help, but because of the black power that Thorgrim neb had put into his spell-casting and cursing, he did not succeed in getting a chieftain to take up with him...he has now been an outlaw for six years." 27

The penal code of Iceland is best illustrated by examining merely one paragraph out of *Guthmundar Dyri Saga*, in which every form of punishment, or combination of punishments, is represented. In the saga, Jon Loftsson tries to settle the feud between Saemundr over Jonsson and Gudmundar dyri, which occurred over the death of Onundr Thorkelsson, who was burned to death. Loftsson assesses fines, lesser outlawry, and full outlawry to the guilty parties:

"The sentences of outlawry were also promulgated at the Althing. The sons of Arnthrud, Thorstein and Snorri had to leave Iceland, one of them to stay abroad for three years and the other never to return, but the final decision on that was left to them. It was also decided that Thord Laufaesing should either leave Iceland for three years or pay a fine of fifteen hundreds; Kolburn had to pay half of this and a half of the weregild for Onund. Both Kolbein and Gudmund were to stay away from their estates for three winters, if they wished, and then the fines would be decreased by five hundreds for each winter of absence from home." 28

The purpose of outlawry was twofold. One, to decrease violent acts in Iceland, as just the threat of being banished so easily would be enough to intimidate someone from committing a crime. And two, to remove the problem from Iceland before it manifested itself in other areas of the country or continued to be a problem in the area the person in question had originally settled. What made this penal system effective was that it was definite. One didn't get off for good behavior. One was outlawed.

Notes

1. H.E. Johnson, "The Old Icelandic Republic," in *Iceland's Thousand Years*, ed. Skuli Johnsson, p. 48.
2. Sigurdur A. Magnusson, *Northern Sphinx; Iceland and the Icelanders from the Settlement to the Present*, p. 23.
3. Ibid.
4. Ibid.
5. Njordur Njardvik, *Birth of a Nation*, p. 37.
6. Magnusson, op. cit., p. 25.
7. *Laws of Early Iceland; Gragas*, trans. Dennis, Foote, and Perkins, introduction, p. 7.
8. Njardvik, op. cit., p. 36.
9. Ibid.
10. Ibid. p.37
11. G. Turville Petre, "Outlawry," p.770.
12. Ibid. p. 769.
13. Ibid.
14. Ibid. p. 770.
15. Jesse Byock, *Feud in the Icelandic Saga*, p. 219.
16. Petre, op. cit., p.770.
17. Ibid.
18. Ibid.
19. *Gragas*, op. cit., p.7.
20. Magnusson, op. cit., p.24.
21. Njardvik, op. cit., p. 37.
22. Johnson, op. cit., p. 48.
23. Byock, op. cit., p. 220.
24. Ibid.

25. *Hoensa-Thoris saga*, trans. Gwyn Jones, p. 33.
26. *Njal's saga*, trans. George Johnston, p. 32.
27. *The Saga of Gisli*, trans. Magnuss Magnusson & Hermann Palsson, p. 165.
28. *The Saga of Gudmundar dyri*, trans. Julia H. McGrew & R. George Thomas, p. 185.

Bibliography

Byock, Jesse, *Feud in the Icelandic Saga*, Los Angeles: University of California Press, 1982.

Gjerset, Knut, *History of Iceland*, New York: The MacMillan Company, 1924.

The Saga of Gisli, translated by George Johnston, Toronto: University of Toronto Press, 1963.

The Saga of Gudmundar dyri, translated by Julia H. McGrew and R. George Thomas, New York: Twayne, 1974.

Hoensa-Thoris saga, translated by Gwyn Jones, Oxford: Oxford University Press, 1961.

Johnson, H.E., "The Old. Icelandic Republic," in *Iceland's Thousand Years*, edited by Skuli Johnson, Canada: Columbia Press, 1946.

Laws of early Iceland: Gragas, translated by Andrew Dennis, Peter Foote, and Richard Perkins, Winnipeg: University of Manitoba Press, 1980.

Magnusson, Sigurdur A., *Northern Sphinx: Iceland and the Icelanders from the Settlement to the Present*, London: C. Hurst & Co., 1977.

Njal's saga, translated by Magnus Magnusson and Hermann Palsson, Great Britain: Penguin Books, 1960.

Njardvik, Njordur, *Birth of a Nation*, translated by John Porter, Iceland: Iceland Review, 1978.

PALE FIRE: ALLEGORY OR ALLEGORICAL?

Having read Thomas Pynchon's *The Crying Of Lot 49*, the student of literature has seen the mechanisms of narrative allegory in action without understanding its goals or defining characteristics. The student recognizes the book's self-reflexive use of language, its obsession with signs, signals, and words as parts of a code that belongs to some unknown order of things.

The student, hoping for an easy conclusion to his or her analytic work, becomes frustrated as he or she realizes that the interpretation of *The Crying Of Lot 49* can go on indefinitely. Parts of the book refer elsewhere in the novel and back again, to outside textual influences, and finally, to the world itself. These things are all defining characteristics of the "genre" of literature known as allegory.

Having read *The Crying Of Lot 49*, then, the student of literature is able to see what narrative allegory is. After being educated in the theory and workings behind allegory, and after reading Vladimir Nabokov's *Pale Fire*, the student is able to see what is *not* narrative allegory but merely allegorical in nature.

In such a brief essay as this, one can only touch upon the essentials of narrative allegory and hope that the generalities of the definition suffice in fulfilling the essay's purpose. Important to the concept of allegory is the allegorical work's *pretext*. The pretext, according to Maureen Quilligan in *The Language Of Allegory: Defining The Genre*, is "that source which always stands outside any allegorical narrative and becomes the key to its interpretability (though not always to its interpretation)" (p. 23). True allegory, Quilligan implies, leads the reader to other texts. *Pale Fire* does not.

Perhaps the most important aspect of narrative allegory is its self-reflexive use of language. Allegory is (and always has been) the most self-reflexive and critically self-conscious of narrative genres; its purpose is to make the reader correspondingly self-conscious" (p. 24). Narrative allegory has as its source a culture's attitude towards language and the limitless possibilities contained in that language. In language and words, the reader seeks meaning and an "order" to things.

"Analogies, patterns, and connections in language mirror similar synchronicities in the cosmos" (p. 150). The role of narrative allegory is to call attention to what Quilligan refers to as the "other" (God or some sacred text), through "interfolded correspondences between word and world." Or, as Quilligan states, "one woven web of sense (one text) calls attention to the plexed (or folded) artistry of another text."

Allegory leads to meaning itself. It leads outside itself to other textual sources and ultimately even outside those sources to the world at large, whose code we can unscramble in order to gain an understanding of the text, the world, and ourselves. "Allegorical fiction is aimed at leading the reader out of the fiction, to a place where he can view himself in relation to his world, seen again in its eternal dimensions, only there, outside himself, in touch with the Other, is man happy" (p.153).

Nabokov's *Pale Fire* fails as allegory because it does not lead outside itself to the "Other," but immerses the reader deeper and deeper in its web of "patterns, correspondences, verbal symmetries, puns, analogies, and mirror words." Nabokov's self-conscious use of language makes this "semblance of a novel" allegorical in nature, but nothing more. *Pale Fire* is parody of allegorical fiction and criticism but, lacking a pretext, fails to achieve the defined status of allegory. With Nabokov, "the mere pleasure of the game is its own reward" (p.153). Nabokov's words do not lead the readers to other texts, nor even outside the book.

Pale Fire is such a perfect parody of allegorical fiction and criticism (intended or not) that perhaps its true purpose is to comment on the folly of allegorical readings. If the case, Nabokov is warning the reader about what may happen when the criticism overwhelms the text, the "apparatus criticus turns into the semblance of a novel."

His text is a critical text in itself, parodying and underscoring the shortcomings of any criticism that threatens to make an author's work its own.

OF ENTROPIC DECAY
AND HIDDEN DEMONS:
THE RICH, CHOCOLATY GOODNESS
OF THE CRYING OF LOT 49

"People think I know more about the subject of entropy than I really do."
—Thomas Pynchon, *Slow Learner*

"…a new mode of expression takes over. It can only be called a kind of ritual reluctance. Certain things, it is made clear, will not be spoken aloud: certain events will not be shown…"
—Thomas Pynchon, *The Crying Of Lot 49*

"Ones and zeroes," something or nothing: *The Crying of Lot 49* is something to be listened to and decoded, or it is a noise to be muffled and ignored. In listening to *The Crying of Lot 49* we must sort out Pynchon's messages from his "noise" and, like Oedipa Maas, decide whether there is meaning or meaninglessness in them.

"Behind the hieroglyphic streets" of Pynchon's world "there would either be a transcendent meaning, or only the earth" (136). The reader must decide on one or the other. There is no middle ground.

To attempt an understanding of Pynchon's world, the reader must become an active participant in the unraveling of clues. What will the reader find? Exactly what Oedipa finds:

"She stared at it in wonder. It was as if she had just discovered the irreversible process" (95). This "irreversible process" is entropy, and for the reader to arrive adequately prepared with Oedipa "to await the crying of lot 49" (138), he or she must have an understanding of entropy and its role to the characters of the novel.

Simply put, though the idea of entropy is not a simple one, "the concept of entropy is a mathematical measure of the disorganization of a system." 1 Obviously, the systems in *The Crying Of Lot 49* are at a high level of entropy.

"The idea first arose as a part of the theory of heat, but a similar notion can be associated with probability distributions of any kind." 2 In *The Crying Of Lot 49*, these probability distributions include the interactions of characters, systems of communication, and the ending of the novel, if it can even be called a "conclusion."

The probability of a given system's tendency to move towards a highly disordered state is high. As entropy increases, the universe, and its closed systems, move from the least to the most probable state, from a state of organization to a state of chaos. Entropy, then, is inevitable, and unstoppable.

When the reader understands this he is capable of "all manner of revelations." Entropy is not only valuable as a tool for uncovering meaning and significance in the book, it is the key to the reading process of the book, and by extension, the confusing maze of our own existence.

Entropy was introduced by Rudolf Clausius in 1852. The basis for the idea of entropy lies in the First and Second Laws of Thermodynamics, which can be stated in one sentence: "The total energy content of the universe is constant and the total entropy is continually increasing. In other words, it is impossible to either create or destroy energy." 3

The First Law of Thermodynamics says that in any closed system, any system theoretically isolated from the rest of the universe, "while energy can never be created or destroyed it can be transformed from one form to another." 4

If we burn a piece of coal, the energy remains but is transformed into sulfur dioxide and other gases that then spread into the atmosphere. While no energy has been lost in the process, we can never burn that piece of coal again because it no longer exists in its original form. 5   The explanation for the loss of the burned coal as available energy lies in the Second Law of Thermodynamics, the law that encompasses entropy:

"Every time energy is transformed from one state to another, a certain penalty is exacted. That penalty is a loss in the amount of available energy to perform work of some kind in the future. This is entropy. Entropy is a measure of the amount of energy no longer capable of conversion into work." 6

The piece of coal has been lost as a possible source of energy in the future. The price paid for burning the coal is that its entropy has increased, resulting in its energy being converted into a product that can no longer be used. In simple terms, this is pollution. "Pollution is the sum total of all the available energy in the world that has been transformed into unavailable energy. Waste, then, is dissipated energy." 7   In *The Crying of Lot 49*, all the characters except Oedipa Maas are represented as closed systems in which entropy is increasing. Clausius observed that in a closed system the difference in energy levels tended to even out and approach the equilibrium state, the state where there is no longer any difference in energy levels. 8 The equilibrium state is the state where entropy is at a maximum. The higher the entropy, the more disorganized and chaotic a system has become.

The characters in *The Crying Of Lot 49* do not resist their own entropic decay or fight against the equilibrium state, and so they appear to Oedipa to exist in a state of chaos and disorder. To bring things back into a state of order requires the expenditure of additional energy. The characters surrounding Oedipa are unwilling to expend the energy needed to return order to their lives and so reach a high level of entropy before their time has come.

All of us are approaching a state of equilibrium, or death, where we can no longer resist our own entropic decay. While we live, we can feed ourselves, maintain our health, learn as much as we can, in a nutshell, we can live. "To be alive is to participate in a continuous stream of influences from the outer world and acts on the outer world." 9   No person is a closed system in the literal sense, but figuratively, a person can close themself off from experiences, information, and communication.

Entropy in communication and information theory is easier to understand than it is when applied to thermodynamics. The more ambiguous a message, the more entropic it is. For instance, if a French man and an American, neither of who speak the other's language, converse with each other, the amount of information exchanged is most likely going to be zero. The entropy of their communication is high, a state of equilibrium has been reached, and no exchange of information is possible. 10

Gain in entropy always means loss of information. The higher entropy there is, the less information a message conveys. Pynchon's message in *The Crying of Lot 49* is that entropy in the closed system of American society is increasing rapidly and that we are experiencing a major failure in communication, an identity crisis that could lead to apocalypse. 11

The level of communication in Oedipa's world is nil. Her relationship with Mucho is characterized by "their inabilities to communicate" (29). When Mucho writes to her, Oedipa has "an intuition that the letter would be newless inside" (30). Oedipa is constantly looking "around for words, feeling helpless " (53), and never finding them. Even the latrine walls at the Tank Theatre are void of graffiti: "She could not say why, exactly, but felt threatened by this absence of even the marginal try at communication latrines are known for" (48). The end result of a society in which even the simplest level of communication does not exist is apocalypse. Without communication, there is nothing but silence.

Failure in communication also manifests itself as "pollution." As stated earlier, waste is dissipated, unavailable energy. Waste in communications is the message that is unavailable for conveying information, a.k.a. noise. Noise results in a total failure of communication. Two people talking in a small, quiet room can easily hear each other's words, but in a crowded room in which a hundred people are talking over one another, those two people will have a hard time hearing each other. Noise inhibits communication. "Noise is any undesirable signal in information theory and corresponds to disorder in the way that a signal corresponds to order." 12 Noise is communication theory's waste, its garbage.

It is no coincidence, then, that the underground organizations uncovered by Oedipa communicate via the W.A.S.T.E. system. The letters Yoyodyne employees exchange through W.A.S.T.E. are void of communication, messages passed as if the participants were just going through the motions of communication, knowing that nothing is being said, no information conveyed.

Oedipa notices this, but fails to see that this notion might apply to all communications in her pursuit of meaning. She continues searching for "The Word," refusing to accept that the messages sent her way might only be so much noise, like when she gets stuck in rush hour traffic on the Bay Bridge:

"Oedipa was appalled at the spectacle, having thought such traffic only possible in Los Angeles, places like that. Looking down at San Francisco a few minutes later from the high point of the bridge's arc, she saw smog. Haze, she corrected herself, is what it is, haze. How can they have smog in San Francisco?" (79).

What Oedipa sees is pollution, but she denies it, trying to convince herself that it is haze. Oedipa plays this role throughout the book, trying to differentiate "smog" from "haze," meaninglessness from meaning. Oedipa becomes a metaphorical Maxwell's Demon, a metaphor in its own way, sorting highspeed molecules from low speed molecules, all in the quest for meaning:

"She did gather that there were two distinct kinds of this entropy. One having to do with heat engines, the other to do with communication. The equation for one, back in the 30's had looked very like the equation for the other. It was a coincidence. The two fields were entirely unconnected, except at one point: Maxwell's Demon.

As the Demon sat and sorted his molecules into hot and cold, the system was said to lose entropy. But somehow the loss was offset by the information the Demon gained about what molecules were where" (77).

J.C. Maxwell proposed his "sorting demon" in 1871 as a challenge to the Second Law of Thermodynamics, the Entropy Law. Maxwell posed the following hypothesis. An "intelligent" being small enough to handle individual molecules would be capable of violating the second law and escape the effects of entropy. Maxwell considered what would happen if, in a vessel filled with gas and divided into two parts, A and B, by a division with a small hole in it, there were an individual (the Demon) who saw the individual molecules and could open and close the hole so as to allow only the swifter molecules to pass from A to B and only the slower ones from B to A.

In this way, without the expenditure of energy, the temperature of B would be raised and that of A lowered, contradicting the Second Law of Thermodynamics. 13 The Demon sorts out the molecules in such a way that energy is produced without expending energy to create it. This theoretically violates the law of entropy.

The Nefastis Machine is a model for Maxwell's theory, making Oedipa a modified Maxwell's Demon, sorting out the clues of Inverarity's will as if they were molecules, some with the potential for creating energy, or meaning, and some creating nothing. "Entropy is a figure of speech, then," sighed Nefastis, "metaphor. It connects the world of thermodynamics to the world of information flow. The Machine uses both. The Demon makes the metaphor not only verbally graceful, but also objectively true" (79).

Oedipa is supposed to stare at the Nefastis Machine and cause a piston to rise by sorting energy-potential molecules from energy-deficient molecules. She must "communicate" with the machine and make it hear her presence. She fails to do this. Either the demon does not exist or she is not able to communicate with it. This is a recurring choice in the book, one that Oedipa must make over and over again.

Oedipa's failure to communicate with the Nefastis Machine might be caused by more than the fact that she lacks the ability to communicate, though. The Demon's ability to avoid entropy is also doubted. Scientists after Maxwell argued that his Demon would not be able to avoid entropy, that it could not create energy without utilizing energy, and that it could not get something for nothing because it must use energy to sort high speed from low speed molecules.

It needs to expend energy to create energy, just as Oedipa must use her energy to draw meaning from her revelations. Oedipa cannot sidestep entropy, she can only fight against it, just as the reader must put effort into, expend energy on, Pynchon's book to get meaning out of it. Nothing comes of nothing. Oedipa knows she is in between two worlds, like the Demon, receiving information about both but unable to sort the faster-moving molecules from the slower. 14 These "molecules" come to Oedipa as clues that seem to come at her by coincidence at first and later as if they have been laid out in front of her to find.

One of these clues is the film "Cashiered" that Oedipa watches with Metzger, the child actor Baby Igor-turned-lawyer. The film within the book is filled with possibly significant implications. The American Heritage Dictionary defines the verb "cashier" as "to make void, do away with," which is what happens to Oedipa by the end of the book.

41

Metzger disappears, giving up his executorship of Pierce's will to the law firm of Warpe, Wistfull, Kubitschek and McMingus. The more Oedipa becomes immersed in Pierce's legacy, the more she is "cashiered" from responsibility towards the estate. The nearer she gets to executing the will, the more it seems to slip away from her. In the end she has become "will-less," unable to do anything but wait for Lot 49's crying.

Entropically, the more energy Oedipa puts into decoding Pierce's will, the less information it conveys. *Cashiered* seems to convey little meaning, which is true, but what it does convey is important. The submarine "Justine" is a closed system, just as the film, that outsiders attempt to "Pierce" through. Oedipa bets Metzger that the submarine and its crew won't make it at the end of the film. In different terms, she bets on the most probable ending rather than an improbable Hollywood ending. 15   Oedipa bets *for* entropy, which is characterized by its high probability.

Indeed, the submarine at the end is punctured, fills up with water and drowns the occupants. The closed system is penetrated and a state of equilibrium in which the water outside the sub reaches a pressure equal inside the sub ensues. Oedipa wins the bet, choosing the most obvious ending.

If she were to continue choosing the most possible endings throughout the book, she might come closer to "the truth," or something close to it. In terms of entropy, it's possible that there is no meaning in any of the clues thrown her way, that no information is being conveyed to her, and that she is seemingly the only "sane" witness to a total breakdown of communication and meaning.

Two other characteristics of the *Cashiered* episode shed light on the role of entropic meaning in Pynchon's world. Metzger's game of Strip Botticelli never leads to the answers of any of Oedipa's questions: "So it went: the succession of film fragments on the tube, the progressive removal of clothing that seemed to bring her no nearer nudity…" (26).

The more clues that are "stripped away" in Oedipa's quest, the further away from the book's nudity, or truth, she and the reader find themselves. Oedipa must take something off for each question she asks, paralleling the obsolete concept of Maxwell's Demon. Each piece of clothing represents energy expended to create energy, or meaning:

"Another earring?" said Metzger. "If I answer that, will you take something off?" "I'll do it without an answer," roared Metzger, shucking out of his coat" (25). Metzger reveals himself here as a victim of his own entropic decay. He does not ask for any information before he expends energy, e.g. takes off his coat. Metzger has become a closed system stricken by equilibrium in which information and identity have deteriorated through entropy. He neither asks for information nor reveals information.

He is forever frozen in *Cashiered* as Baby Igor, which has confused his identity, leaving him to adapt to the filmic extension of himself. 16 As entropy increases, the universe and its closed systems lost their distinctiveness to move from the least to the most probably state, from a state of organization and differentiation to the most probably state, from a state of organization and differentiation in which distribution and form exist, to a state of chaos and sameness. 17

A second level of meaning is implied by the *Cashiered* segment of *The Crying Of Lot 49* having to do with Umberto Eco's third type of labyrinth, the net. The main feature of a net is that, "Every point can be connected with every other point, and, where the connections are not yet designed, they are, however, conceivable and designable. A net is an unlimited territory.... a net has neither a center nor an outside." 18

Every point in the book leads to another point and back again, which explains why Oedipa never uncovers the one "epileptic Word." She is exploring an unlimited, infinite territory that is, to make things worse, characterized by its entropic lack of information. "One thing we can do," announces Baby Igor's father before he gets "cashiered," "go to the bottom, try to get under the net" (19).

It is impossible to get under the net with hope of finding anything more meaningful than exists above it. Under the net, Oedipa only discovers a further web of loosely connected connections, an underground network of closed system organizations all loosely related in some way to the mysterious "Trystero."

A second "entertainment" within Pynchon's main show that contributes further towards our own understanding of the forces of entropy in the book (or an understanding of why we don't understand) is *The Courier's Tragedy*. Pynchon's parody of Jacobean Revenge Tragedy suggests a parallel between a Jacobean society facing its extinction and today's society as it faces its own potential extinction.

It is interesting to note that the Oxford Companion to English Literature's description of revenge tragedy's common ingredients include: 1.) the hero's quest for vengeance, often at the prompting of the ghost of a murdered kindred or loved on; 2.) scenes of real or feigned insanity; 3.) a play within a play. Perhaps Pychon constructed *The Crying Of Lot 49* with some of these ingredients in mind.

Oedipa is forced into a quest of sorts by the death of a loved one. Pierce's ghost figuratively haunts her throughout the book. Oedipa bounces back and forth, as do most of the characters she runs into, between real or feigned insanity." By the end of the book, neither Oedipa nor the reader is able to discern the difference between the two states of mind.

The Courier's Tragedy is the play within Pynchon's own main play. It "was being put on by a San Narciso group known as the Tank Players, the Tank being a small arena theatre located between a traffic analysis firm and a wildcat transistor outfit..." (44). Again, entropy is referred to, as the Tank, like Maxwell's Demon, is stuck between thermodynamics and information, circulation and communication, traffic analysis and transistor production.

The Courier's Tragedy is itself based on the themes of circulation: the circulation of mail and the destruction of communication by diabolical forces. Entropy is the common denominator of the two. Thomas Pynchon sees a parallel of entropic decay in the communication systems of the Jacobean Age and the present in which Oedipa witnesses the dissipation of all lines of information around her. From the play, she catches a fleeting glimpse of a message, a meaning, a system that she might be able to apply to the events taking place around her, perhaps even explain and reverse the "irreversible process:"

"Oedipa found herself after five minutes sucked utterly into the landscape evil Richard Wharfinger had fashioned for his 17th century audiences, so preapocalyptic, death-wishful, sensually fatigued, unprepared, a little poignantly, for that abyss of civil war that had been waiting, cold and deep, only a few years ahead of them" (44).

She is not, however, able to generate a meaning with which to interpret the unraveling of the world around her. The play points somewhere, but does it point to meaning, to an explanation? Things will not be made clear for Oedipa. She glimpses significance in the play, but it resists her with its "ritual reluctance. Certain things, it is made clear, will not be spoken aloud; certain events will not be shown onstage" (49).

It is the same "ritual reluctance" that all clues Oedipa pursues come equipped with. They allude to the generation of zero information, like the character Randolph Driblette plays, Gennaro, who *generates zero*. In the course of the play, Pasquale "dies in extreme agony, and in marches Gennaro, a complete non-entity, to proclaim himself interim head of state" (48). Gennaro, in fact, is the only one (or zero) left alive at the play's conclusion when Pynchon describes him as the "colorless administrator" (53).

Who are these people that seem to play such important roles in the play (and the book) yet have so very little to convey in the way of significant meaning? Like Gennaro, who generates nothing, zero. And Richard Wharfinger, whose last name is defined as "the owner of manager of a wharf." In his name, the reader sees a wharf *finger*, a jetty or pier that points like a finger out into the deep. 20

And what about Randolph Driblette, who follows the playwright's pointing finger into the deeps of the Pacific Ocean. The O.E.D. (and OEDipa Maas would agree) defines a *driblet* as "a petty or inconsiderable quantity or part of anything; in petty portions at a time; little by little; in '*driblets.*'"

Driblette seems to tell Oedipa little or nothing in his conversations with her, but perhaps he tells more than Oedipa comprehends. Pynchon, of course, is the "God" of his book, the invisible force behind everything that happens beneath (and in) his created world's net. It is in these characters (who seem to tell Oedipa and the reader the least) that Pynchon reveals himself the most. Randolph Driblette is Thomas Pynchon.

Oedipa goes backstage to talk to Driblette after the play, where "She couldn't stop watching his eyes. They were bright black, surrounded by an incredible network of lines, like a laboratory maze for studying intelligence in tears. They seemed to know what she wanted, even if she didn't" (54).

Oedipa finds herself face to face with her Creator. He hypnotizes her, makes her forget why she came backstage, knows what she is really looking for, "even if she didn't," yet Driblette/Pynchon tells her, or so she thinks, nothing. If he does have anything to tell her, he exits the book before Oedipa can talk to him again. But doesn't Driblette/Pynchon tell Oedipa, and in the process, the reader, *about* nothing?

Driblette's words in the scene following *The Courier's Tragedy* stand out as the potential key that will unlock meaning in the book, and point the reading process of the novel at the same time:

"You came to talk about the play," he said. "Let me discourage you. It was written to entertain people. Like horror movies. It isn't literature, it doesn't mean anything. Wharfinger was no Shakespeare" (54). And neither is Pynchon, who warns against looking too deeply into *The Courier's Tragedy* in particular, and *The Crying Of Lot 49* in general. "Why," Driblette/Pynchon said at last, "is everybody so interested in texts?" (55)

Why indeed:

"You can put together clues, develop a thesis, or several, about why characters reacted to the Trystero possibility the way they did, why the assassins came on, why the black costumes. You could waste your life that way and never touch the truth. Wharfinger supplied words and a yarn. I gave them life. That's it" (56).

We, as readers, can never have a complete understanding of what *The Crying Of Lot 49* really means. Only Thomas Pynchon knows this and he, like Driblette, conveniently disappears before we can get to him for an explanation:

"You know where that play exists, not in that file cabinet, not in any paperback you're looking for, but-" a hand emerged from the veil of shower-steam to indicate his suspended head-"in here. That's what I'm here for. To give the spirit flesh. The words, who cares?....But the reality is in *this* head. Mine. I'm the projector at the planetarium, all the closed little universe visible in the circle of that stage is coming out of my mouth, eyes, sometimes other orifices also" (56).

Driblette/Pynchon refers to the stage as a closed system that he controls. He is the "sorting demon" who decides what molecules of meaning make it through the door and into the minds of his audience. He decides what Oedipa will know. He decides what we as readers will know. If it is not much or nothing at all then we are supposed to understand that our ability to communicate has been and is still failing.

If we are too concerned with *how* it is being said rather than with *what* is being said, then we are not listening. Because we try to apply meaning to Pynchon's language in *The Crying Of Lot 49*, we miss the point that his language is communicating nothing and that it is meant to leave us feeling confused just as the failure of communication confuses us.

We cannot bring Pynchon's novel "into pulsing stelliferous Meaning" (58) as Oedipa wishes to bring the world around her into some sort of significance. Oedipa becomes confused, catastrophically so, because of language's failure to adequately make her understand. She learns nothing from the entropy-doomed systems of communication around her because they no longer have anything to tell, or have forgotten how to tell it.

If Driblette/Pynchon sees some message in *The Courier's Tragedy*, he is unable or perhaps unwilling to share it with Oedipa. The message he sees in the play might be his way of dealing with the entropy of communication around him. Others in the book deal with the entropy of communication in their own ways. Some succumb to it and perish, literally in death, figuratively in insanity.

Metzger never transcends Baby Igor and runs off with a nymphet. Mucho drops acid and crosses over Hilarius's "Bridge Inward." John Nefastis reaches a state of equilibrium with the television world in which he immerses himself. The members of Inamorati Anonymous kick the love habit to avoid getting hurt. Hilarius, whose sanity was to be doubted in the first place, goes nuts, steeping in paranoia.

Each of us must find our own way to deal with the entropy of communication because, like death, in Pynchon's worldview, it is inevitable. The end result is that all of us will become closed systems fighting against the state of equilibrium for as long as we can. The end result of this is an "anarchist miracle," "some unthinkable order "of music, many rhythms, all keys at once" (97), in which no collisions take place because everyone has become closed off from everyone else.

Oedipa spends most of the book, as do we, "waiting for the collisions to begin" (97), waiting for communication, waiting for the message. But none come. There are no collisions, there is no communication, only apocalypse when each person has become closed off from everyone else. The entropy of communication will inevitably continue until there is no longer communication.

Searching for meaning in Pynchon's words transforms us into Maxwell's Demon, trying to escape the effects of entropy, trying to sort out meaning from the "noise" around us without putting our own valuable life's energy into the effort. But the "sorting demon" cannot get by the effects of entropy, and neither can we. The reversal of the entropic death of all communication is impossible. There is only increasing entropy, disorder, and ambiguity.

The final page of *The Crying Of Lot 49* leaves Oedipa Maas locked in yet another closed system: "She heard a lock snap shut; the sound echoed for a moment" (138). We, as readers, are inside the room with her. For the first time in the book, we are *inside* a closed system. The door is shut and locked and we still cannot escape the effects of entropy.

We picture "Loren Passerine, on his podium, hovering like a puppet master, his eyes bright, his smile practiced and relentless. He spreads his arms in a gesture that seems to belong to the priesthood of some remote culture; perhaps to a descending angel. The auctioneer clears his throat. We wait for the crying inside that we hope will abolish the night's screaming outside. We settle back, to await the crying of lot 49."

Notes

1. Whitrow, G.J., "Entropy," *The Encyclopedia of Philosophy*, vol. 2, 236.
2. *ibid.*
3. Rifkin, Jeremy, *Entropy: A New World View*, p. 33.
4. *ibid.*, p. 35
5. *ibid.*
6. *ibid.*
7. *ibid.*
8. *ibid.*, p. 36.
9. Abernathy, Peter, "Entropy In Pynhon's *The Crying Of Lot 49*," Critique, 14, 2 (1972), p. 29.
10. *ibid.*, p. 20.
11. *ibid.*, p. 29.
12. Plater, William, *The Grim Phoenix: Reconstructing Thomas Pynchon*, p. 55.
13. Whitrow, *op. cit.*, p. 326.
14. Plater, *op. cit.*, p. 57.
15. Lewicki, Zbigniew, *The Bang And The Whimper: Apocalypse And Entropy In American Literature*, p. 91.
16. Abernathy, *op. cit.*, p. 28.
17. *ibid.*, p. 20.
18. Eco, Umberto, *Semiotics And The Philosophy Of Language*, p. 81.
19. Kermode, Frank, "The Use Of Codes," p. 72.
20. Cowart, David, *Thomas Pynchon: The Art Of Allusion*, p. 105.

Bibliography

Abernathy, Peter L. "Entropy in Pynchon's *The Crying of Lot 49*." Critique, 14, 2 (1972): 18-33.

Cowart, David. *Thomas Pynchon: The Art of Allusion.* Carbondale: Southern Illinois University Press, 1980.

Eco, Umberto. *Semiotics and the Philosophy of Language.* Bloomington: Indiana University Press, 1984.

Kermode, Frank. "The Use of Codes." In Seymour Chatman (ed.), *Approaches to Poetics.* New York: Columbus University Press, 1973.

Lewicki, Zbigniew. *The Bang and the Whimper: Apocalypse and Entropy in American Literature.* Westport: Greenwood Press, 1984.

Plater, William M., *The Grim Phoenix: Reconstructing Thomas Pynchon*, Bloomington: Indiana University Press, 1978.

Pynchon, Thomas. *The Crying of Lot 49.* Philadelphia: J.B. Lippincott, 1966.

Rifkin, Jeremy (with Ted Howard). *Entropy: A New World View.* New York: The Viking Press, 1980.

IS IT ENLIGHTENED SIMULATION OR SIMULATED ENLIGHTENMENT?

"Saigon, November 1967" 'The animals are sick with love.' Not much chance anymore for history to go on unselfconsciously." —Michael Herr, *Dispatches*

"To dissimulate is to feign not to have what one has. To simulate is to feign to have what one hasn't. One implies a presence, the other an absence."
—Jean Baudrillard, *Simulations*

What purpose does the academic paper serve in a simulated society? Within a simulation such as we are immersed, according to Baudrillard, is not the academic paper a simulated response to a simulated world? Why must we submit a written document such as this to receive a grade? The very act of writing for a grade implies that the document is an accumulation of all knowledge assimilated in a given course. This might not be so.

The paper might only be a well-assembled simulation of accumulated knowledge that gives the impression of learning when in fact it may only reflect the student's recognition of what the professor wants to see and hear. Is the student an enlightened student or is he a simulation of an enlightened student?

If he is enlightened, as Habermas would encourage him or her to be, the academic paper is a real reflection of that student's learning. If the student is simulating an accumulation of knowledge to get a good grade in the class with no consideration for real knowledge or enlightenment, he or she has succumbed to the hyperreality of Baudrillard's order of simulacrum. The very act of writing this final paper reflects the incompatibility of Habermas and Baudrillard. It does not appear that a belief in one leads to an equal belief in the other.

To accept Habermas's idea of a continuing enlightenment, one must deny Baudrillard's idea of a world without the real, a world in which the model of the real is more real than the real itself.

Baudrillard's world of hyperreality reveals a world without reference points common to more than one person. There is no common reality. There is no common sense of history. There is no reality. There are only simulated models of reality that have been mistaken for and interpreted as the real. If there is no real, as Baudrillard suggests, then this missing real must spill its influence over all aspects of daily life, including the academic world.

Without the real, what is the purpose of this paper if it is only a simulation of the knowledge accumulated in the course of this course? What is the point, except to receive a simulated grade, a sign with no meaning, and a degree in the mail, another sign absent of all meaning?

Habermas argues for the continuation of the Enlightenment in our lives today. If we associate Habermas's theory with Baudrillard's, and it appears that we must associate the two in some way, we are left with either simulated enlightenment that bears no relation to actual real enlightenment, or we create the act of enlightenment as a conscious recognition of the absence of significance in the signs around us.

There exists, then, either enlightened simulation or simulated enlightenment. Are these two choices really the extremes of the state of the real or are they incompatible as theoretical mates? Both theories, while dissimilar in their content, are parts of the same basic narrative of existence. They are two different ideas from two different men with two different realities, but they are linked at the humanistic level.

That is, they are at least associated by species, and in class, the two are part of the overall narrative of History 100. To link the two is to, perhaps mistakenly, link them together at the locus point of a common reality. This would contradict Baudrillard's theory in which the world finds itself in a disintegrative period of "cool" homogenization.

Reality is defined by no longer having the time to happen; thus there is no time to build a link between Habermas and Baudrillard's ideas. In a world of simulation there is nothing to find. There are no connections to be made because there is nothing that is real enough to have any association with anything else that is as real as it is. Nothing else is as real as that which it is a simulation of. Everything is self-referential. There are specialized groups of thinkers with specialized groups of realities. There is no common sense and there is no common reality. The image, the idea, the thought bears no relation to any reality. With this in mind, Baudrillard's words become nothing more than the model of a theory with no common sense of a frame into which we can paste them alongside the words of Habermas. There are only individual canvasses. There are no collages.

The collage becomes an isolated simulation of togetherness, of oneness between the individual objects within the frame. The collage becomes a *one* with no relation to any other *ones*. There is no relation between the two, hence, there is nothing, or zero, zilch, nada between anything, as Pynchon suggests in *The Crying of Lot 49*:

"She had heard about excluded middles; they were bad shit, to be avoided; and how had it happened here, with the chances once so good for diversity? For it was now like walking among matrices of a great digital computer, the zeroes and ones twinned above, hanging like balanced mobiles right and left, ahead, thick, maybe endless. Behind the hieroglyphic streets there would either be a transcendent meaning, or only the earth. Ones and zeroes. So did the couples arrange themselves" (p.136).

The coupling of Habermas and Baudrillard into some semblance of commonality is absurd to even attempt. In terms of Baudrillard, that is. If Baudrillard is conscious enough to perceive the absence of the real in society, then he has become enlightened to the very society he discards as disintegrative. If anything, Baudrillard's own enlightenment must be real, though real only in his reality.

54

Our reading of Baudrillard's enlightenment cannot give us a full understanding of Baudrillard's life force but it can lead us to a conscious enlightenment of our own. It can lead us to examine our own state of the real, of "our" real, and though it may be unlike the real that our next door neighbor is experiencing, we are enlightened to its state of non-existence. Baudrillard, if anything, is guilty of Habermas's proposed enlightenment. His use of the "art" of literary and historical criticism promotes his and our "understanding of the world and of the self, moral progress, the justice of institutions and even the happiness of human beings" (*The Anti-Aesthetic*, p.9), which, ultimately, were the goals of the Enlightenment.

The world may be based, tragically, on the simulation of the real, but Baudrillard's promotion of his ideas as the state of postmodern society reveals that enlightenment is not dead. The language used to describe the real, perhaps, has grown more convoluted. Enlightenment has become more complex than it was before. New experiences and ideas can be interpreted and examined in terms of hundreds of different theories, of which Habermas's and Baudrillard's are only two.

Carlos Castaneda implies a second order of language utilized in his induced states of hallucinogenic reality in *The Teachings of Don Juan: A Yaqui Way of Knowledge*:

"I wanted to comment on the strange quality of the water, but what followed next was not speech; it was the feeling of my unvoiced thoughts coming out of my mouth in a sort of liquid form. It was an effortless sensation of vomiting without the contractions of the diaphragm. It was a pleasant flow of liquid words."

In a world of simulations, even the hallucination is real. It too is a model of reality, or a model of non-reality from which Castaneda, and perhaps others who study his writings, can draw enlightenment into their own lives. Is this simulated enlightenment or enlightened simulation? There is nothing to distinguish the two from one another. Does it matter?

All one can do is try to make sense of his or her own particular reality. Baudrillard, apparently, has dealt with the world around him by postulating the death of the real. By inducing the reader to look at the world in terms of the hyperreality it has turned into, Baudrillard incites the reader to enlightenment.

Habermas encourages us to put reason and rationality into the world. Enlightenment means that we are supposed to act on our present by making sense of it, by understanding our role in the now, which is always the only time that is happening to us. The now is the only moment in which we actively participate. It is the only time that we can truly act upon. The past is unchangeable. The future is unpredictable. Habermas suggests that the past that is characterized by the ideas advanced by the enlightenment is still active. The future we are incessantly moving towards must exist in the reason created by the past. Historical consciousness gives us a sense of direction.

Enlightenment is the same thing as historical consciousness. If we understand where we have come from, we can rationally attempt to understand what the future will be like. We can attempt to make our present continuous with the past and our future continuous with our present.

The enlightened individual recognizes that in life and throughout history there is good and there is bad. Habermas suggests that it is enlightenment to acknowledge all positive and all negative aspects of society. There are great writers and poets and there are struggling artists who are never heard from on the face of this earth. As Charles Bukowski writes in *Tales of Ordinary Madness*, "GREAT POETS DIE IN STEAMING POTS OF SHIT."

At the same time, the enlightened individual will recognize the fact that while Habermas's theory is one way to look at reality, there are other theories that examine the idea of reality in different ways. In this sense, the individual must not only make the historical past continuous with the history of the present and the future. He or she must also make the literary past continuous with the literary and critical present. In this way, Habermas's "Living Enlightenment" can be conciled to Baudrillard's Third Order, the order of unrestrained exchange and simulation. For Baudrillard, there is not a true and honest recognition of the past as a tool to make our present clear to us. History means nothing to us if we cannot stockpile it in museums, on television, and in history books:

"Ramses means nothing to us: only the mummy is of inestimable worth since it is what guarantees that accumulation means something. Our entire linear and accumulative culture would collapse if we could not stockpile the past in plain view" (*Simulations*, p.19).

There is no history except the simulation of the past. The past is dramatically recreated for television. Napoleon's horse is stuffed and put behind a window for ages to come. Lenin is stuffed and put on exhibit in Red Square. Dinosaurs are resurrected. But they are lifeless incarnations. Is this really such an outrageous practice as Baudrillard makes it out to be?

Without museums, without television, without books, there would be no documentation to prove to our psyches that the past actually happened, that Lenin and the dinosaurs were once real.

This seems harmless enough, but danger lies in the potential misinterpretation of the simulation of history by the individual to be the real:

"Simulation is no longer that of a territory, a referential being or a substance. It is the generation by models of a real without origin or reality: a hyperreal" (p.2). Baudrillard suggests a substitution of signs of the real *for* the real: "Illusion is no longer possible, because the real is no longer possible" (p.38). The only possibility is simulation when historical simulation is perceived as historical reality.

It follows that in a society based on simulation, other signs, images and ideas turn into nothing more than models of their real counterparts. Where does the simulacrum end? Does it end? Or does it take on new forms of simulation as we pass into the future of technological advances sure to come?

Inevitably, there can only be an entropic implosion of meaning. If simulation becomes the norm, the real becomes the abnormal. Abnormalities are weeded out, and all that will remain is the hyperreal. There is no way to save the real if it has already been overcome by the hyperreality of simulation.

There is some hope, though vague, in the potentials of Habermas's enlightenment. It is possible that a return to order in society rather than the simulation of order can be achieved by continuing the ideas of the enlightenment. With this movement, we turn towards the rationality of enlightened simulation rather than the homogenization implied by simulated enlightenment. The real may never be restored but recognition and awareness of the hyperreal and its simulacrum is not too hard to imagine if there is a serious examination of what is "live" and what is "Memorex."

If we understand that an image is only a simulation it cannot touch us in the way that it can if the difference between them is not made clear. Perhaps this is an idealistic concluding note, maybe not. If education has succumbed to the hyperreal, there may be no way to reconcile the two in such a way that the individual living in postmodern society can distinguish one from the other.

For Baudrillard, it is already too late to reverse the irreversible process of entropic decay that has burned away the base of the real. Education may not be able to reverse this process, but Baudrillard's enlightened simulation shows that the historical critic has not entirely succumbed to the simulacrum. Baudrillard recognizes the decay of the real. He, at least, has not been swallowed by the hyperreal in such a way that he has become blind to it.

Baudrillard's role, then, is to enlighten the unenlightened. It is his job to warn us. By reading Baudrillard, shadowy ideas without names become concrete observations rooted in the postmodern context. What begins as an idealistic hope for education to be the differentiating factor between the real and the model of the real disintegrates into wishful thinking if Baudrillard's ideas are already integrated into the postmodern world:

"Never again will the real have to be produced—this is the vital function of the model in a system of death, or rather of anticipated resurrection which no longer leaves any chance even in the event of death. A hyperreal henceforth sheltered from the imaginary, and from any distinction between the real and the imaginary, leaving room only for the orbital recurrence of models and the simulated generation of difference" (p.4).

It is impossible to educate an individual to distinguish between the real and the model of the real because the two have become one. As Baudrillard states, "What society seeks through production, and overproduction, is the restoration of the real which escapes it" (p.44). Reality is evading us more and more as time goes by and nothing can save it from dissipating altogether.

Or, Baudrillard argues, it already has.

WHAT'S GOING ON?

We want to be soothed but if you really look at the world there doesn't appear to be much soothing to be had. Look back over your year. No, I don't mean *your* year, I mean *the* year. Do themes exist? Do we really pass through phases of time that can be defined with "meaning" or is everything as out of control as it mostly appears to be?

I bought a bike this summer, the first one I've owned in more than ten years. I thought it was just the Seattle rainy seasons that had made me soft, but now I know it was the lack of a bike. From my apartment, the whole world is downhill. This makes for exhilarating departures, but to get back home it's always uphill, and that's a different story. I notice after two months of riding that I now take the downhill rides in stride. They're fun, I like the speed and exhilaration, but it's the uphill ride I'm hungry for now. A newspaper article in front of me says that the universe will go dark in a few trillion years. I've heard this before, but tonight I am trying to really *comprehend* this fact.

If we don't do ourselves in over the course of future years, the universe will eventually do it for us, so does it really matter what we do with our lives, with the planet? Is it this silent knowledge in our subconscious that causes us to appear to be a suicidal human race, always on the brink?

No wonder: we live inside a light bulb: no matter what we do we'll always be on an uphill ride. One day down the line our ancestors are going to watch the light fade. Will they figure out a way to escape this demise?

My brother had a baby this summer, which must have led to this dream: a vision of every child born before me that led to my existence, and every child born after me *because* of my existence. I saw them stretched out behind and in front in an infinite line streaming far out into space.

We really aren't individuals, but part of some strange liferay we haven't fully learned how or where to aim. We've never cared much about communicating with our future selves; perhaps we need to start this process.

I was sitting at the computer one night this summer when the power went out. I felt…inconvenienced. After a few minutes of sitting in the dark, I got on my bike and rode out to see what was going on. It took me a while to reach the streets that had light, and when I found them I realized that I wanted to be back in the dark.

It felt like I was cheating with my plan to go to a bar and read a book, so I lit the cheesy peace sign candle I'd bought at the dollar store as a joke and listened to the night. I couldn't believe how quiet it was without the hum of television, internet, stereo. It was…comforting. A few weeks later, the power went out in New York and all up and down the East Coast. An article in the newspaper detailed ten suggestions from Iraqi citizens about how to deal with no electricity, air conditioning, and water.

A picture in the *New York Times* at the beginning of the war in Iraq showed soldiers sitting in an armored personnel carrier waiting to go into combat. The soldier in the middle of the picture was holding a bag of Skittles. Later, I read an article that said Pop Tarts were much sought after among the troops and that the makers of numerous products had signed exclusive contracts with the military to guarantee their wares were eaten and used as part of Desert Storm.

Then there was the little detail in an account of the shootout that led to the demise of Sadaam's sons Oday and Qsay about what was found in the room where they made their last stand: a bloody mattress, a can of Pepsi, and a box of Mars Bars, their last meal. Mars: closer to Earth this summer than it has been in 60,000 years. Staring up at it from behind my friend's house one night, it really did look "close." More often than not this past summer, I found myself wondering, "what is going on?"

Next year, the last of the *Star Wars* saga will be released. Most younger people I've talked to think the *Star Wars* films "suck." It's hard to explain what it was like when the first one came out in 1977, that films back then stayed in theatres for months, not weeks, and that they weren't released with matching snacks.

I'm curious to see how people react to Darth Vader embracing the dark side of "the force." Leave it to George Lucas to muck it up, but think of it: the hero of this film is a villain. Are dark days ahead? Are these dark days we live in now?

In Glencoe, Scotland, there is a place called The Island Of Discussion. In the old days, if you had a disagreement with someone, you were sent to the island with food and water and were expected to stay there until you worked out your quarrel. Perhaps we need such an island today. An Island Of Answers.

SCIENCE IS THE NEW ART

The news is not good: suicide bomber on a bus in Israel; suicide bomber outside a subway station in Moscow; beheading of one Nepalese hostage and execution by bullet to the head of twelve others in Iraq.

I've grown used to these headlines, but last night's quick succession of images at the top of the BBC news caused me to sigh a sigh that took me a few minutes to decipher. Resignation? No, it felt more like, "enough already, we get the point."

Images of the bus bombing were familiar: twisted wreckage, brief shots of the injured, men placing body parts in plastic bags. These in quick succession were followed by the surprising image of the bus being driven away. Not towed, *driven*. Despite the fact that its carriage had been blown apart, the bus was still in working condition.

Images from the suicide bombing in Moscow also contained surreal nuances. The female bomber had intended to blow herself up on a train or subway, but turned from the station as she approached when she saw some policemen and exploded her belt bomb in the street. It looked like a beautiful, late summer dusk. The camera crew arrived before any bodies were covered or taken away. The bomb was packed with nails and bits of metal.

To the left, face down on the grass, an old man lay dead. He could have been taking a nap, but for the red circle on his short sleeve shirt. There was a shopping bag next to him. He died walking home from the store. On the right side of the screen, a hundred feet down the street, the shape of another person dead on the ground, their body splayed at a different angle compared to the old man's, and then a shot of a woman, her leg injured, laying calmly on her side in the middle of the street as someone treated her. Her face didn't look shocked or surprised. From the images shown, you could infer the bomb's circular blast pattern. Absent was the mess in the center that would have been what was left of the suicide bomber.

Last week's news briefly showed what remained of another female suicide bomber in Israel. The middle of her body was gone. A policeman raised her head and looked at her face. The news has trained me to expect certain images to accompany certain events; I found these images to be…new…and therefore disturbing.

We are all exposed to the same images and worn down into states of sedation, resignation, survival. Only something we haven't seen before can jolt us, and we have seen everything, or so I thought.

This morning, a group of Chechen rebels have taken control of a school and are holding hundreds of children hostage. I try to imagine what is taking place in the school as I write this. They have gone too far. Leave the kids out of it. The story is unfolding. Perhaps there will be more to report by the time this goes to print, but I have a feeling it is going to end badly (it did).

One could argue that nothing has changed in a year, for better or worse. One might also argue that things have gotten worse. Or, and this is the possibility that we really need to come to grips with, everything is just as it has *always* been.

In the midst of this chaos of news, I have been grappling with the novels of Michel Houellebecq. Houellebecq writes beautifully ugly novels about the beauty and ugliness of the contemporary world. There is too much recognition of our helplessness in the face of instinct and biological programming in his novels to feel very assured or uplifted, but in the end there *is* something strangely reassuring and uplifting about Houellebecq.

I read *Whatever* straight through, *Platform* over two days, and *The Elementary Particles*, his densest novel (and possibly the culmination of ideas explored in the previous works) in just a few straight readings.

There is something very raw, very real, and very *wrong* in Houellebecq's depiction of our contemporary world, so wrong it feels "right." The page-turning quality of his prose and plots aside, Houellebecq goes to the core of issues of racism, consumer society, the "decline of Western civilization," the rise of religious fundamentalism in the face of scientific and technological advance, society's obsession with youth and aging, violence, television, cuisine, psychiatry, and sexuality. In other words, a brutally honest version of what has come of thousands of years of human evolution.

Houellebecq's novels are disturbed and disturbing. *The Elementary Particles*, which you should read last after digesting the first two, achieves an epic scope by its final pages that leaves you wondering about the future fate of the human race.

If you're not paying attention, it's business as usual in the world, but if you *are* paying attention, you should be noticing that *everything is in play*, everything is turning and changing before our eyes. It all seems a little bit out of control, exhilarating and horrifying at the same time.

Never has it seemed like so much is at stake. What exactly that "so much" is, though, will depend on who you talk to and where you stand in your own global views. I noticed a word being used repeatedly in the news: sovereignty. Perhaps it points to what's at stake.

I found its dictionary definition contradictory, its *concept* unclear: 1.) a: Supreme power, especially over a body politic. b: Freedom from external control; AUTONOMY. 2.) One that is sovereign; especially an autonomous state.

How can a word encompass both being a supreme power *and* autonomous? Ambiguity abounds. In "Maybe Not," Cat Power sings a lullaby of resigned defiance: "we all do what we can / so we can do just one more thing / we won't have a thing / so we've got nothing to lose / we could all be free / maybe not with words / maybe not with a look / but with your mind."

Maybe it's better to listen to Colonel Kurtz tell it the way he sees it in *Apocalypse Now*: "It's impossible for words to describe what is necessary to those who do not know what *horror* means. Horror. Horror has a face, and you must make a friend of horror. Horror and moral terror are your friends. If they are not, then they are enemies to be feared..."

Sovereignty. Autonomy. Terrorism. The War On Terror. Threat Assessment. Suicide bombers. Freeedom. This is the vocabulary of our times.

They say this war is going to be with us for a long time. Are you prepared? Are you pulling the strings or are the strings pulling you? Round and round it goes, where it will stop, nobody knows.

Robert Duvall as Colonel Kilgore in *Apocalypse Now*, seemingly relaxed on the beach as shells explode around him, a hint of nostalgia in his eyes, offers his own version of a lullaby: "Some day this war's gonna end."

THE FUTURE

The future isn't what it used to be. It's here, NOW, all around, and we pretend that we are not in awe. People are LIVING in space! You can look up at night and see the space station pass overhead.

The Space Station!

Imagine trying to explain the world to someone from the distant past. They would not understand, nor would we know how to explain how any of it works.

With all of this FUTURE all around, we are still trapped beneath the usual mediocrities of violence and lethargy.

We need an epic journey to crystallize the world's tired imagination. A long time ago, we set out in ships across the sea for places we could only hope existed.

One day, the stars. For now, musings and nostalgia for the future. If you are a time traveler, come get me and take me with you.

TWO: FEELING

HENRI ALAIN-FOURNIER:
LOST AND FOUND IN THE LOST DOMAIN

Born in 1886 in a small French town, Henri Alain-Fournier wrote one published novel in his short life, *Le Grand Meaulnes*. Translated variously over the years as *The Wanderer*, *The End Of Youth*, *The Lost Domain*, and now *The Lost Estate*, the book captures the dream-like quality of moments that later resonate as symphonies of memory and loss, nostalgia and regret.

Anyone tortured by a haunted past might want to think twice about reading this book; those who revel in such musings and who possess even a strand of the *fin de siecle* concept of romance should seek out *Le Grand Meaulnes* immediately.

While not strictly autobiographical, the author's life and the novel mirror each other in numerous ways. At the age of eighteen, Alain-Fournier visited an art exhibit in Paris.

After leaving the museum, he encountered a young woman whose aura and beauty captivated him. He followed her onto a *bateau-mouche* for a short ride down the Seine to her house on the Boulevard Saint-Germain, and began returning frequently to sit beneath her window.

On one of these occasions a curtain parted and the woman, Yvonne de Quievrecourt, smiled at him. One afternoon he was at last able to speak to her, according to most accounts for no more than an hour; she revealed that she was scheduled to leave Paris the next day and to be married. On parting, she turned and looked at him for what he describes as a long time before disappearing. "Since then," he wrote to her in an unsent letter, "I have never stopped searching for you."

Although Alain-Fournier continued on with his life and education, he remained obsessed with his memories of Yvonne. In 1913, his younger brother discovered that Yvonne's family owned a house in Rochefort, and arranged for Henri and Yvonne to see each other. During this second and last encounter, he showed her the unsent letter in which he wrote, "I cannot resign myself to not finding you again, to never setting eyes on you."

Now married with two children, she admitted that during a rough patch in her marriage, "I thought of you all the time. I would have written if I had known how to…but now I'm the happiest of wives."

A year later, during a battle near Verdun, the 28-year-old Lieutenant Alain-Fournier was seen firing his pistol while running towards the German lines, and was never seen again.

In between his fateful meeting with Yvonne and his demise, Alain-Fournier composed and published *Le Grand Meaulnes*.

The story of the novel centers around two characters: the young Augustin Meaulnes, a rebellious instigator who arrives in a small French village to attend boarding school, and Seurel, the schoolmaster's son, who narrates and reflects on the book's events, acknowledging soon after Meaulnes' arrival that he "was counting on him for some extraordinary exploit that would be sure to turn everything upside down." His new friend fulfills this youthful desire and more.

Meaulnes gets lost after setting out on a solo adventure and comes upon a mansion in the woods, where he encounters a beautiful woman named Yvonne during what comes to be known as "the strange party."

The next morning, exhausted from the night's dream-like events, Meaulnes hitches a ride on a departing carriage and falls asleep while trying to memorize the path that led him there. When he wakes, he has no idea how to find Yvonne or the location of the mansion.

He returns to tell Seurel of his adventure; the rest of the novel deals with their search for the lost domain, and what happens after one finds it. Children at the beginning of the novel, Meaulnes and Seurel grow up but are never fully able to leave the events of their youth behind.

Alain-Fournier's novel isn't only about the sense of regret and lost moments, though; it is also about that age when we sense there are adventures in store for us, and search for them without a thought of the possible consequences. The reader becomes a willing accomplice when Seurel muses that he is:

> "searching for something far more mysterious. It is the path told of in books, the ancient obstructed path, the path to which the weary prince could find no entrance. It is found at the last forlorn hour of the morning, when you have long since forgotten that eleven or twelve is about to strike…and suddenly, as one thrusts aside bushes and brier, with a movement of hesitating hands unevenly raised level to the face, it appears in sight as a long shadowy avenue, the outlet of which is a small round patch of light."

In thinking about the possible location of "the lost domain," Seurel goes on to say "that in front of me, far from Meaulnes, far from all hope, there had just opened out, as clear and easy as a familiar road, a path to the manor without a name."

Alain-Fournier's novel is a detailed map to this manor with no name, the place where wonder converges with reality to endow singular moments with the substance known as poetry.

What more could you want from a novel?

Sources consulted:

Towards The Lost Domain: Letters From London, edited by W.J. Strachan (Carcanet Press, 1986)

The End of Youth: The Life and Work of Alain-Fournier, Robert Gibson (Impress Books, 2006)

Afterword by John Fowles, *The Wanderer* (Signet, 1971)

PAUL LEPPIN: THE LIGHT IN DARKNESS

Paul Leppin's dark novels should not be read in spring, when the days are long and full of bloom. His perfect, twisted little book *Severin's Journey Into The Dark* and the doubly twisted *Blaugast: A Novel Of Decline* are meant to be read by candlelight in the deepest nights of winter. Or perhaps one *should* approach Leppin's dark work beneath the watchful eye of the sun, both for the sake of one's sanity and because Leppin is the sun's dark cousin.

Where the sun brings light to the world, Leppin revels in exploring the strange light that exists in the depths of his characters' depraved souls. Blaugast is a clerk who abandons himself to sensual self-destruction. Stricken with a heavy melancholy and malaise—one that reflects the mystical squalor of Prague circa 1900-1930, which Leppin vividly depicts—Blaugast suffers both physical and spiritual fevers caused by his journeys into the dark.

In the opening scene of the book, an old school friend invites Blaugast to a seamy bar where he meets the prostitute Wanda. She immediately casts a spell on him and takes over his life. The tone of both the book and Blaugast's temperament are set when Leppin writes, "Fate had come to Blaugast out of the tunnels of night. An apocalyptic woman had seized him...like a lifeless stone, he sank to the bottom, into the throes of sex, into the insanity of his fate, into the sleep of the damned."

Wanda arranges sexual choreographies for Blaugast, which leave him so stricken that he is no longer interested in going to his job or being part of the everyday world. Wanda then turns Blaugast into her servant in his own apartment while she services the men who bring her money now that he has none to offer. He lets his physical appearance go, begs for offerings on the street, is given the nickname "Little Baron" and asked to "do the bird" by the denizens of Prague's nightlife that Leppin describes so well. Blaugast obliges, hops and squawks, aware now that "he had become a peddler of his own corruption."

The single ray of light in the book is Johanna, a prostitute who discovers a connection with Blaugast, but she too is a dark light shining on a dark world. If, in the end, Blaugast is a love story, then it's certainly not the kind mainstream Hollywood would ever produce. Still, there are revelations and scenes of strange and twisted beauty in Leppin's narrative, where "life isn't all glitter, even for the fortunate," where "there grows no hedgerow separating misery from eternal bliss," and where "the pangs of love are indestructible, and for everyone the same."

RAYMOND RADIGUET'S
BOUQUET OF FLAMES

Bouquet of flames (which stolen / kisses make more bright)
--Raymond Radiguet, "Bouquet Of Flames"

It is spring, it is summer, it is autumn, it is winter. You find yourself in the mood for love, romance, or coarse ecstasy. You should read Raymond Radiguet's novel *The Devil In The Flesh*. It is spring, it is summer, it is autumn, it is winter. You find yourself recovering from heartbreak, disappointment, or craving more of what you tasted before it slipped away. You should read Raymond Radiguet's novel *The Devil In The Flesh*.

Written between the age of 16 and 19, The *Devil In The Flesh* was published in March of 1923. Radiguet died in December from typhoid fever not long after completing his second novel, *Count D'Orgel's Ball*. He was twenty years old. Of that final novel, Jean Cocteau wrote, "it is frightening to see a child of twenty publish a book that can't be written at that age." His statement seems more applicable to the author's first book. Radiguet's second book is like a spider web in progress. *The Devil In The Flesh* is pure venom.

According to Martin Turnell in *The Rise Of The French Novel*, the book was apparently inspired by real-life events: "…as early as 1912, when he was only nine years old, Radiguet wrote something like a love letter to one of his teachers at the primary school… The liaison began in 1917, the year in which Alice like Marthe in the novel married a soldier who was home on leave from the front and who is known in the novel as Jacques, when she was nearly twenty-five and Radiguet only fourteen—ages changed to nineteen and fifteen in the novel."

The novel's narrator is an unnamed "I." While he describes the external action of his experiences with Marthe in great detail, the real action of the novel takes place in his mind as he meditates on the nature of love and its various phases, summed up by three key quotes.

"Like the first taste of a strange fruit, my first kiss had been something of a disappointment," he muses at first, "We derive our greatest pleasures not from novelty but from familiarity. A few minutes later I had not only grown accustomed to Marthe's mouth—I could not do without it."

Ten pages later, coming to terms with the anxieties his love incites, he observes, "we think we are the first to experience such anxieties, not realizing that love is like poetry, and that all lovers, even the most ordinary, imagine themselves to be innovators."

Further along, he revises and questions his affection: "All love has a youth, a maturity and an old age. Was I already at that final stage when love no longer satisfied me unless accompanied each time by some new trick?"

The book is filled with many such observations that make the reader pause and think about their own experiences in the realms of romance and heartbreak.

Count D'Orgel's Ball, published after Radiguet's death, also centers around a triangular affair between a young man and a married woman, but instead of fully-realized romance, the book is about the resistance of desire in the name of preserving friendship and conjugal love; all the heated moments of this novel take place in its characters' minds.

The book is cluttered, suffering from too many minor characters and too much backstory about them, which stalls Radiguet's prose that so forcefully propelled his first book forward. Similar moments of insight are present here as well but are fewer and further apart, and while the book's thematic nuances will resonate with some readers, one reads this book looking but not finding echoes of the crystalline first.

Rounding out Radiguet's contributions to literature is a slim volume of his collected poems, *Cheeks On Fire* (out of print). The author describes them as "the natural expression of a blend of reticence and a hiddenness proper to the age at which they were written," and suggests the collection "...can throw some light on an obscure age—the age proper to ingratitude: sixteen, seventeen, and eighteen years old. At that time, months have the value of years."

Narcissus, Venus, the ocean, and angels make numerous appearances, as does the same knowing eroticism present in the novels. These lines from "Venus Unmasked" serve as an accurate depiction of the writer's character and perhaps also as an appropriate epitaph to his body of work:

"Goddess, admit / that a teen-aged novice belies your tale. / I'm really not impressed by your boasts / because you've taught me how to read / the booming waves, those soft maternal / wrinkles on the ocean womb. / But I'll repay you as befits / an artless youth: since you let me enroll / as a pupil in your risky school / I'll teach you how to read my soul."

As for Radiguet's short literary life, it is summed up best by Aldous Huxley's epitaph in his introduction to the 1969 Bantum edition of *The Devil In The Flesh*: "Radiguet set out in possession of those literary virtues with which most writers painfully end. In what ways would time have further ripened this precocious maturity? We can only sadly speculate. Radiguet was still a boy when he died."

THEODORE ROETHKE: "THE LONGING"

In his poem "The Longing" from North American Sequence, Theodore Roethke uses image clusters to create a triptych of a soul's despair, desire and awakening. The poem's narrator begins the poem "an eyeless starer," using a list of miseries to illustrate how his soul is fatigued and empty.

Roethke uses two primary image clusters in the first part of "The Longing" that place the narrator's soul in a hellish landscape of waste and rot. The first cluster is made of "a kingdom of stinks," "fetor of cockroaches, dead fish," "saliva dripping," "agony of crucifixion on barstools." These in turn lead the narrator from spiritual unconsciousness to a partial awakening from the fatigue of lust when he asks himself, "How to transcend this sensual emptiness?"

A second cluster of images only confirms what was revealed in the first and fails to lift the spirit from its "half-life." This second cluster of images comes in the poem as a cloud of heaviness weighing the narrator's spirit down, keeping it from rising up against its own malaise: "In a bleak time, when a week of rain is a year," "slag-heaps fume," "gulls wheel over their singular garbage," and "not even the soot dances." Nothing, not even soot, is allowed or able to achieve a state of lightness. Everything is heavy, the spirit "shrinks back into a half-life, less than itself, "a slug, a loose worm," "an eyeless starer."

The second part of "The Longing" is dominated by images of "a dark dream," as "a body with the motion of a soul" allows its spirit to be awakened by its own wretchedness, solitude and nothingness. Roethke uses three dominant images to lead his narrator away from the dregs of his soul to an awakening from which "all beginnings come:" "the rose," "the moon, and "a great flame" rising from "the sunless sea."

The narrator points out that, "the rose exceeds us all;" it is an object of perfect beauty. And finally, the disastrous state of the narrator's soul is revealed after "a great flame rises from the sunless sea: "he is "there to hear" its light, there to be awakened from his spirit's descent into malaise, but he is so far removed from spiritual fulfillment that he is beyond even the moon. Its beauty does not stir him, but the realization that he is "bare as a bud, and naked as a worm" allows him to see that his spirit is "free; how all alone. Out of these nothings—All beginnings come."

In the third part of Roethke's poem, the narrator transcends his state of spiritual bleakness through the awakening of his longing "for the imperishable quiet at the heart of form." The key word in this part of the poem is "would." "I would" this, the narrator says, "I would" that. His longing to be awakened leads him to make a list of desires that might enable him to free his spirit. Roethke uses a dominant cluster of images from nature to illustrate the narrator's awakening: "the fish, the blackening salmon, the mad lemmings," "children dancing, flowers widening, "a stream," and "a leaf." These are all images of the "redolent disorder of this mortal life" that transcend their mortal fates by achieving lightness "where shadow can change into flame, and the dark be forgotten."

In the last ten lines of "The Longing," Roethke uses images to illustrate the narrator's acceptance of the natural state of decline and death that is part of nature, not man-made rot and waste, but part of the natural order of things: "the dead buffalo, the stench of their damp fur drying in the sun, the buffalo chips drying." This last set of images allows the narrator his firm epiphany. He will not just be an explorer, looking at things, discovering them and moving on. He will be part of the natural order of the earth, one with the things around him, and he will celebrate both the light and the dark spaces in his spirit because nature itself is filled with light and dark, order and chaos, birth and death, growth and rot.

JOHN BERRYMAN: "HE STARED AT RUIN"

Dream Song number forty-five reads like Henry's death warrant. As if looking down at a piece of paper he is about to sign, "He stared at ruin. Ruin stared straight back." The word "Ruin" becomes a character's name in this *Dream Song*. Ruin is a character in Henry's life. "He thought they was old friends," but they are not, they are like old lovers who don't want to have anything to do with each other but keep coming back for more. Henry thinks, for a moment, that "he had/the knack of ruin," since their paths cross so frequently and since ruin is so familiar to him.

This *Dream Song* employs syntax of negative confirmation. Everything Henry thinks he is positive about in this *Dream Song* turns out to be what he is completely unsure of, and everything he is sure of, ruin, will only lead to his ultimate negation, a confirmation of ruin. "He thought they was old friends," Berryman writes, then, later, "they were not old friends." But then a stranger appears, "come to make amends for all the imposters, and to make it stick." He is positive that this one, *this* Ruin, will Ruin him for good.

Berryman uses repetition in this *Dream Song* to underscore the recurrence of Henry's engagements with ruin. Ruin is repeated twice in the first stanza. Their paths "cross" six or seven times in the second stanza, and "this one" is used twice in the third stanza. Ruin, in all its guises, is the familiar stranger in Henry's life. It crosses his path again and again, until finally, real Ruin arrives to stay for good, to un-Henry Henry, nodding hello to his end.

SEAMUS HEANEY: "STATION ISLAND"

Presences, glimpses, and sensations of things felt to be near but far away at the same time wind their way through each section of Seamus Heaney's poem "Station Island." One has the sensation that the poem's narrator doesn't know whether to believe in these presences that are there but not there, as if every one of them is endowed with an aura of holiness that calls into question his ideas of faith. Section Six of "Station Island" introduces the narrator's vision, a nameless but nicknamed girl/woman he describes as, "Freckle-face, fox-head, pod of the broom, catkin-pixie, little fern-wish" and who arouses and awakens his senses. There is no way to know how present she ultimately is or was in the narrator's life since the poem seems to boil down to a remembrance of a glimpse of this vision and the Dante-esque emotions stirred in the narrator's mind as a result.

Heaney works all of the senses but touch into this part of the poem in response to her beauty. Sight: "I was sunstruck," "I saw her honey-skinned shoulder blades and the wheatlands of her back." Sound: "dunes where the bent grass whispers," "I shut my ears to the bell," "a somnolent hymn to Mary." Metaphorical, but to the narrator, very real sensations of taste: "my own long virgin fasts and thirsts, my nightly shadow feasts." Smell: "a window facing the deep south of luck opened and I inhaled the land of kindness."

The third stanza of section six emphasizes the nature of worship that is inseparable from the narrator's sight of his vision. The keyhole image ("As if I knelt for years at a keyhole/Mad for it") suggests a mad monk hungry for divine intervention, a meeting with God, confirmation of His existence. As if the narrator has prayed for and received the miracle of seeing his vision's "honey-skinned shoulder-blades and the wheatlands of her back," he becomes a believer when he glimpses the "land of kindness."

He must turn to Dante, though, to find words for the sensations awakened within him: "So I revived in my own wilting powers/And my heart flushed, like somebody set free." He translates these lines under an oak tree. They are the translation, also, of the experience of seeing his ideal of beauty fulfilled in the real world. One can only hope that the word "given" in the last line means that the narrator was able to give these lines to his vision and not share them only with old pangs of lost desire and the readers who experience the poem and remember their own long lost visions.

JOHN ASHBERY: "OFFSHORE BREEZE"

John Ashbery's collection *April Galleons* is filled with a tone of wistful solitude, an almost gentle loneliness, and a meandering yearning for some primordial empty space to be filled with...what?

One has the feeling that Ashbery is writing towards this space, this hole, this absence that prevents the mind from being whole, but his tone of loneliness is never one of violent upheaval or disillusioned disgust.

His poems are journal entries of an almost mystical wanderer. They are never bitter but always filled with a melancholy that constantly plays itself against the Day of Judgment, as in "Offshore Breeze," in which the narrator suggests that one can nap until that day arrives, "Or can one?"

"What happens is you get the unreconstructed story," he writes, "An offshore breeze pushing one gently away, not far away." The narrator's voice suggests he has taken notes on his journey but that it is for us to fill in the empty space he makes available for us to explore.

He also questions his own awareness when he says, "Perhaps I have merely forgotten, Perhaps it really was like you say. How can I know?" All that is sure is that, "life grows increasingly mysterious and dangerous with nobody else really visible."

"Offshore Breeze," like many of Ashbery's poems, is a veiled love lyric, not too demanding of its object of desire but ever aware of his/her presence in the world. At the end of the second stanza, after his musing on the Day of Judgment, the narrator admits, "I like you because it's all I can do."

In the meantime, though, he writes poems, in the middle of which are these muted lines of longing, held too long in the mouth: "And he spat out the pit."

Desire spoils when held too long without release.

C.K. WILLIAMS: "REGRET"

The collection *Flesh And Blood* gave me the feeling of a voice both detached and involved with the world, in the wings as well as the street. Williams is like Rainer Rilke, Pablo Neruda, or Roberto Juarroz descending from the spiritual heights for a look at what goes on near the gutter, on the news, and in other people's lives, after which he returns again and again to the machinations of his own soul, where he can say, as in the poem "Regret," "I am the life and was the life, to dying say I am still the matrix and again the fire."

It is from this matrix, this fire, that Williams emerges to describe "the way" of the observed worlds he sees and his involvement, body and soul, with that world, so that, in the space of the page and a facing page, his voice moves like a cinema panning shot that takes in a junior high school concert, a young Elizabeth Bishop, two gigantic teddy bears on the bumper of a pick-up truck, and the old regret that is worse than death.

Williams would rather "die than live through dying with it: rather perish absolutely now than perish partially in its cold coils which would mean savaging the self from far within where only love, self-love, should be allowed to measure what one was and is and to roll the bales of loss aside." This regret is one source of the poems in *Flesh And Blood*, one place they arrive from where the self doesn't malign itself thinking about what "was not endured but was accomplished."

These poems are miniature statues, monu-moments to what is endured throughout life and what, in the end, is accomplished.

DEREK WALCOTT: "SUMMER ELEGIES"

Lost love and ruin always seem to be more interesting in poetry than the happy lines that celebrate love's more glorious manifestations. The aftershock of love's ruined landscape is territory familiar to everyone. We can all relate to the blues and to love gained and lost, as in Derek Walcott's two-part poem "Summer Elegies." The first part reveals Walcott in the La-La land of love with Cynthia, feeling love, "could renew itself, and a new life begin," as they "made one shape in water while in sea grapes a dove gurgled astonished 'ooos' at the changing shapes of love."

Changing shapes indeed, as part II of the poem finds Walcott musing on Los Angeles, pain, and losing Cynthia. Walcott associates the city's landscape with the pain of unfinished business. "Nothing hurts as much as the word 'California,' the wincing light of Los Angeles," he writes. Walcott's love, like Los Angeles, appears to have been as superficial and short-lived as "the poetry in roof-wide ads for the latest release, the billboards plugging a Sony, a new way to live, ours, we were sure, a second-best bet, a Hertz or an Avis; now so many songs have California in them, and the H in Hollywood hurts."

Walcott repeatedly uses words invoking temporality to underscore the nature of his involvement with Cynthia: "unfinished Venice," "a fresco interrupted in its prophecy looks phonier that what it promised," "the false fronts, the fake Spanish facades" that he "understood." A few stanzas later, Walcott tries to joke about his short-lived affair: "I must smile, or die, hence this lightness. Hence this fake chic, these stanza windows like a posh boutique in a semitropical desert." Then the jokes stop and the sad emptiness of an empty studio lot after the filming is over sets in: "West Venice changes its gels for the fade. We become, said Borges, books when we are dying." The death of Walcott's love, though, grants him no such mercy, and there is no such mercy for any of us. When love dies, there is nothing but its death to fill in the empty space. Our love dies and we share Walcott's fate: "I died and did not become any book in the city of angels" where there are no angels of mercy, only pop songs with reminders of lost love and more pain "than all of Cambodia."

MADNESS AND LOVE, SURIN AND BRETON

"I confess I am hesitant to take this leap, fearing a fall into some endless unknown."   —Andre Breton, *Mad Love*

The quest for love is madness but, as Maurice Blanchot writes in "The Madness Of The Day," "I wanted to see something in full daylight; I was sated with the pleasure and comfort of the half light; I had the same desire for the daylight as for water and air. And if seeing was fire, I required the plenitude of fire, and if seeing would infect me with madness, I madly wanted that madness."

Is Love madness or is madness one end result of passion gone awry? The individual craves an outlet leading to the place, person, and state of mind where he or she can lower their guard that has been raised against the invading madness of each day gone by without love, without passion, without the knowledge of another being, another world.

Michel de Certeau's essay "Surin's Melancholy" presents a strong case for the necessity of madness and love in the life of the passionate individual, specifically the madman/mystic Jean-Joseph Surin, whose writings serve to allegorize the artistic process of exit from this world into an alternate plane, as well as the fact that love and madness are one in the same, though from opposite sides of the same sphere.

De Certeau suggests that writing serves as an outlet from the interior world of the individual to the outside world. This outlet allows Surin to transcend his madness by channeling it into a focused stream of productivity. Paralysis and fear are traded for words and words become the signifiers of love. Love, then, is made real, is made to exist through the process of transcendence in which the author's passions are leveled out from their former state of virtual or realized hysteria into a realm of realizable potential and grounded reality, not the jumbled flight of broken discourse. De Certeau's biographical sketch and analysis of Surin's melancholia can be linked with Andre Breton's Surrealist exposition of the necessity of The Other, of love, of mystery and the unconscious in *Mad Love*. Surin's madness ultimately finds itself transformed into poetry and a transcendent state of calm in the world. Breton's path moves through a similar forest. "Such beauty," Breton writes, "cannot appear except from the poignant feeling of the thing revealed, the integral certainty produced by the emergence of a solution, which, by its very nature, could not come to us along ordinary logical paths. It is a matter—in such a case—of a solution which is always superior, a solution certainly rigorously fitting and yet somehow in excess of the need. The image, such as it is produced in automatic writing, has always constituted for me a perfect example of this. In just such a way, I have wanted to see some very special object constructed in response to some poetic fantasy."

The Surrealists recognized the reality of the unreal, the consciousness of the unconscious, and they harnessed their powers in their writing and processes of discovery. Michel de Certeau's rendering of Seventeenth Century notions of madness are not so different from Andre Breton's aesthetic notions of the poetic structure built into the poet's unconscious. "According to seventeenth century conceptions," de Certeau writes, "an individual with melancholic or hypochondriacal madness persistently combines an image (an "idea" or "dream" which is in itself neither true nor false) with an affirmative judgment ("I am" the thing I imagine or dream). The madness consists in the tenacity of the judgment and the logical conclusions the melancholic draws from it. But with the conviction of being damned, something quite different is at play; it concerns consciousness itself, consciousness as something excluded from the real, thrown outside it, kept at a distance, a stranger to the world of the signified. Or, in the language of religion, something set out on the doorstep of the real, of God, abandoned and rejected by Him. Of course, existing as refuse in this way, living in a fallen state, still allows the subject to retreat into an "interior" where knowledge of the world grows as one's own being falls into decay."

The Surrealists (and later in the 1960's, The Beats) embraced this notion of madness as a norm in their respective aesthetics. To The Beats, the idea of being "Beat," of being "Beaten," "Beaten Down," led to poetic states of being, realization and transformation, to "Be-At" the moment where the noise of an internal madness is heard in the outside world as words on a page in poetry and prose. "You only have to know," Breton writes, "how to get along in the labyrinth. Interpretive delirium begins only when man, ill-prepared, is taken by a sudden fear in the forest of symbols. What attracts me in such a manner of seeing is that, as far as the eye can see, it recreates desire. How can you resist the hope of calling forth the beast with miraculous eyes, how can you stand the idea that, sometimes for a long time, it cannot be brought out of its retreat?"

Madness was embraced by the Surrealists as a poetic norm. The key to poetic freedom lies behind the door of the unknowable that, given words to describe itself on paper in the world of the real makes itself known by revealing itself to the seeker who is not afraid to embrace its gaze.

Surrealism is nearing its eightieth birthday. Its notions are old, its effects are now part of popular culture. Does this mean that our current tastes in media and the myths produced by the unconscious are based on an ancient form of madness that has been updated and integrated into artistic norms? It would appear so.

"In the unfolding of melancholia," de Certeau writes, "which during the Renaissance was a characteristic of genius, the totalization of the observed coincides with the nothingness of the observer. At this extreme, what is in question is the very discourse which consciousness produces—a discourse hounded from the real, absolute, unbound, and reduced to being nothing in all that it speaks of. From this point of view, the thought of damnation is the elucidation and agony of the exclusion from which the subject's faculty of speech originated. Thus Surin writes, in his consciousness he did not judge it mad to believe he was damned." The curse of visions and moments of unreality are the poet's angelic charms, his or her tools that the writing self to reach the exterior of the page, the word, the world.

Surin's idea that he had been "damned," if placed in the context of his approach to a realization of poetry, the assault against the senses of the interior world's struggle to assimilate a connection to its other can today be seen as the realization of a poetic aesthetic. The poet is not damned with words, he or she is damned with the inability to externalize the internal language that courses through his or her brain, but is also gifted with poetic sensibilities to come to terms with his or her inner and outer worlds. If Surin had lived in Twentieth Century Paris, his madness would have been invited into the Surrealist's salon.

"This image," de Certeau writes, "will seem like only a hollow thought to others, like a dream my mind made up, because the natural, common sense upon which our faith is built bolsters us to such a degree against these things of the other life that, as soon as a man says he is damned, the others judge that it is only madness. But madness is ordinarily in the ideas someone conceives, and even more naturally it is something like hypochondriacs have. They are all the same: one will say he is an idiot, another will say he is a cardinal. These ideas are legitimately held to be mad. But what Father [Surin] said was not like that. Surin quotes mystics to prove his point: "This is not madness, but extreme suffering in the spirit."

"What I have wanted to do above all," Breton writes, "is to show the precautions and the ruses which desire, in search of its object, employs as it wavers in pre-conscious waters, and, once this object is discovered, the means (so far stupefying) it uses to reveal it through consciousness." Desire can spur action, and it can cause paralysis. Desire is veiled as madness but can also be unveiled and revealed to be love or lust.

Passion is a source of inspiration as well as a source of anguish. The love object, be it a person in the world or a poet's constantly sought ideal poem and ideal reader, is a trigger of many jangled nerves in the brain's complex fibers. According to de Certeau, when Surin views the procession of the Blessed Sacrament from his window in Bordeaux, he is stricken with a "deep terror" and "fright:" "it 'seemed to me that an operation occurred in my mind, functioning as intellectual vision, in which I thought I saw Jesus Christ in the Eucharist, in the form of an armed man throwing thunderbolts at me.' The "attraction" that "makes one look" meets an angry gaze that strikes it with lightning. The tangible object within the field of love suddenly becomes a Viewer who, rising up from the back of the picture (as in certain paintings), towers above the onlooker, and in a fury transforms him into something seen."

Foucault describes a similar state of being in *Madness and Civilization* when he writes, "it is not unheard of that the passions, being very violent, generate a kind of tetanus or catalepsy such that the person then resembles a statue more than a living being." The passions induce a coma-like state of consciousness in which the unconscious is separated from its conscious counterpart. The lover is unable to cross the bridge between his desire and the desired. The poet is unable to write. His lines stop where the unconscious erects its strange wall. For the unrealized poet, as in the case of Surin, this phase of alienation from the other, the exteriority of the real, becomes the source of damnation.

His seventeenth century sensibilities tell him that God has abandoned him. The poet in the Twentieth Century says that he is out of touch with his "inner self." Strategies are created to bridge the distance between inner and outer world. Breton introduces automatic writing and writing in trance states. Jack Kerouac embraces a similar venting of inner sounds onto the blank page in "Essentials of Spontaneous Prose:" "Begin not from preconceived idea of what to say about image but from jewel center of interest in subject of image at moment of writing, and write outwards swimming in sea of language to peripheral release and exhaustion." The passion of writing without restraints unleashes poetry from the inner to the outer. The inner self finds its place in the world of the real. The unreal, the source of madness, longing, and poetry, is freed of its unknowability, is given words, named and realized.

Where passion induces paralysis, it also leads to action. "There comes a moment in the course of passion," Foucault writes, "when laws are suspended as though of their own accord, when movement either abruptly stops, without collision or absorption of any kind of active force, or is propagated, the action ceasing only at the climax of the paroxysm. Whytt admits that an intense emotion can provoke madness exactly as impact can provoke movement."

Passion as a source of poetry can induce the capture of the poem, enabling the poet to transcend his wordlessness by moving the noise of his inner voice into the reality of the page. Passion as a source of longing can inspire the lover to almost automatically pursue the object of his or her desire. Desire leads to the realization of the object of desire as being something, someone, connected to the outer world, linked to the seeker's interior in such a way that the inner life is given an outside reality to dwell.

And so Surin is finally drawn from his madness into the world of signs. His poetry "turns the 'I' into an empty space, which the last stanza then fills with a worthy name, the signifier of the other—the name of Jesus:

"My only remaining wish is to imitate the madness
Of Jesus, who one day on the cross,
For his pleasure, lost both his honor and his life,
Relinquishing all to save his love.
It is one to me whether I live or I die,
All that I ask is for love to remain with me."

The pleasure of losing oneself is perhaps what initiated the process, marked by alternating periods of exaltation and depression, which allowed Surin slowly to regain his faculties." Surin had a discussion with a priest who took his confession one day. "I must tell you," the priest told Surin, "that I have often had the impression, coming neither from my imagination nor from my own senses, that before you die our Lord will have the mercy to let you see that you are mistaken... and I hope that you die in peace.' These words had a strong impression on me." After the priest left, "I pondered whether it was actually possible that our Lord could have mercy on me.... Then I heard in my heart these vital words pronounced by our Lord....'Yes, it is possible! These words, spoken inside me, gave my soul life and revived it."

In the months to come, Surin would begin to write again after a long period of being unable to move his pen across the page: "His hand begins to move across the paper. The "interior" finds an "outlet" allowing it to escape its confinement. The excluded becomes embodied and appears on the outside." The "madness" of poetry acts as a cure for the madness of the soul and mind. A body of work appears in the world. Its health and vitality replace the sickness of the soul and mind. The body is rejuvenated. The mind is excited. This is the poetic ideal, the ebbing and flowing process of occurrence and recurrence.

"At the forefront of discovery," Breton writes, "from the moment when, for the first navigators, a new land was in sight to the moment when they set foot on the shore, from the moment when a certain learned man became convinced that he had witnessed a phenomenon, hitherto unknown, to the time when he began to measure the import of his observation—all feeling of duration abolished by the intoxicating atmosphere of chance—a very delicate flame highlights or perfects life's meaning as nothing else can. It is to the recreation of this particular state of mind that surrealism has always aspired, disdaining in the last analysis the prey and the shadow for what is already no longer the shadow and not yet the prey: the shadow and the prey mingled into a unique flesh. Behind ourselves, we must not let the paths of desire become overgrown."

Michel de Certeau concludes his essay by overcoming meaninglessness. He introduces the notion of the name, in Surin's case, his writing which exteriorizes the inner self in conflict with itself: "With the aid of this name, the meaningless can always be overcome, for there is, there must be, somewhere (God) some meaning from which we are excluded or which escapes us." Andre Breton and the Surrealists embrace the mystery of this "meaning" which can be revealed through the act of writing, of "revealing." "The name has the power to construct a body," a body of work.

"Love is indeed at the heart of Surin's poetry. On one level, to love is to die of pleasure, it is a "mad" linkage between 'loss' and 'pleasure.[1] Thus Jesus, in Surin's song, For his pleasure, lost both his honor and his life/Relinquishing all to save his love." Love and the freedom of the soul to roam are at the heart of the Surrealists as well.

"If You Love Love, You'll Love Surrealism," an early Twentieth Century slogan proclaimed in Paris when the movement began. Madness was embraced as poetry. The quest for love, then, is not as mad as it seems. It is a quest for artistic or spiritual clarity in which the cluttered inner self achieves a state of outer calm. The inner self is balanced with the outer.

"All that I ask is for love to remain with me," Surin says.

"I want you to be madly loved." Breton answers.

FORM AND CONTENT
OF A TORTURED SOUL

To understand Samuel Daniel's sonnet #45 from *Delia*, one must examine the nature of its narrator. Imagine a person so unhappy with his life that sleep is his only pleasure, and waking consciousness an unbearable torture. Perhaps the narrator is involved in a frustrated love affair, the object of his affections knowing nothing of his love for her. Perhaps he is dying and has become bitter at the world because it will go on without him. Perhaps he is disillusioned with his life.

Whatever the cause of his daily pains, the narrator paints a dark picture of depression and examines the contrasting nature of night and day, light and darkness, and life and death. Daniel uses personification, a significantly important rhyme scheme, and alternating line patterns to stress the nature of the life the narrator seemingly can no longer bear to live.

It is in the first quatrain of Daniel's sonnet that personification is used, with the narrator addressing sleep as he would a living person. To the narrator, sleep is the "son of the sable Night, / Brother to Death, in silent darkness born." Not only is sleep a living entity, it also has relatives, its father "the sable Night" and Death its brother.

The narrator addresses sleep like a sick patient asking his doctor for relief, begging him to "Relieve my languish and restore the light." Just as the doctor might prescribe some drug to ease his patient's pain, the "Care-charmer Sleep" is most likely to return the narrator to his much-favored world of unconscious bliss.

It is in the schematic structure of Daniel's sonnet that the contrasting differences between night and day are emphasized. The sonnet's Shakespearean rhyme scheme (ababcdcdefefgg) is utilized and it is in the rhyming words of each line that considerable symbolic significance is placed. Looking at the final rhyming words alone, the reader sees the disillusionment the narrator is expressing as well as his emphasis on the differences between the worlds of day and night.

In lines one and three, the final rhyming words are "night" and "light," an obvious contrast between day and night, the waking hours of consciousness and the time at which the world is meant to be asleep. Another such contrast is in lines two and four, where "born and "return" are set against each other. One is "Born" into the world every morning and "returns" to the unconscious world of dreams every night (and eventually, in death's permanent grasp).

While most of the remaining rhyming words express the narrator's feelings of loss and disillusionment (mourn/scorn, vain/disdain), there is a more significant meaning placed in two of the remaining rhyming pairs. In lines six and eight, "youth" and "untruth" are paired. The narrator sees his "shipwrecked" youth as a lie from which he can never escape, and would rather not be constantly reminded of this when he is awake.

Along same line of meaning, "desires" and "liars" are paired up in lines nine and eleven. The narrator, just as he has been betrayed by the falsehoods of his youth, is also betrayed by his desires, which he can only deem as unattainable lies. And finally, reflecting the narrator's desire to be asleep in the grip of Death's brother rather than confronting his life and working to improve it, is the rhyming pair in lines ten and twelve, "morrow" and "sorrow." With the coming of the day's light, there will only be feelings of loss of control and regret. To wake up in the morning is to suffer, and rather than do this, the narrator would sleep forever.

The alternating lines of the sonnet reflect the similarly alternating nature of day and night, the theme that recurs over and over throughout. In lines three through fourteen an alternating line scheme is used, with alternating images of light and dark, day and night, included in each. Line three has the narrator asking sleep to "restore the light," while line four mentions the "dark forgetting of my cares." Lines five and six are contrasted in a similar manner, with "let the day be time enough" placed against "the shipwreck" of the narrator's youth.

In line seven, Daniel's subjects of action are "waking eyes" while line eight mentions "the night's untruth." Again, positive vs. negative, light vs. dark. This is most obvious in lines eleven and twelve, where line eleven contains the image of a "rising sun," usually a symbol of hope and optimism for the new day, while in line twelve, "grief," "aggravate," and "sorrow" are emphasized. For the narrator, the rising sun brings only another day of torture. He is obsessed with the nature of life and death, the tragedy of his problem-filled life, and seemingly would rather sleep forever than greet each new day as an opportunity to better himself and his view of the world.

Since the reader can only conjecture at what has led the narrator to arrive at this dismal state of mind, it is possible that things in his life really are as bad as depicted. If this is the case, then perhaps the best we can do is wish him the sweetest of dreams that last forever.

THE NATURE OF LIFE, LOVE, DEATH, AND COMMITMENT

The nature of unrequited love is examined in John Donne's "The Canonization" and Robert Herrick's "His Return to London." While the subject of Donne's poem is the love between the poet and his mistress, Herrick's poem is about the love between the poet and his native city of London. Though these are two different types of love, love for a person and love for a place, both are equal in magnitude of feeling and passion.

In both poems, it is implied that each narrator's better days are behind them. Donne speaks of "my palsy, or my gout/my five gray hairs, or ruined fortune," while Herrick's narrator states, "Weak I am grown, and must in short time fall." Both have nothing to lose in asking the subject of their affection to accept their love.

Donne's narrator begs his mistress to "For God's sake hold your tongue, and let me love." He does not want her to deny him at least an explanation of his love, he wants her to accept his love as it is, and perhaps even love him back. He asks her in an almost desperate tone "Alas, alas, who's injured by my love?"

Herrick's exiled narrator expresses a similar plea to London upon his return: "London my home is: though by hard fate sent/into a long and irksome banishment;/Yet since called back; henceforward let me be." He asks, as Donne's poet asks, for no more than his love to be accepted.

Both narrators go on to examine the nature of their commitment to the thing they love. Herrick's narrator looks at this commitment based on the physical characteristics of the city and the fact that it is the place of his birth. He addresses the creator of such a city with the refrain "O fruitful genius! that bestowest here/An everlasting plenty, year by year."

The narrator could ask for no more from a place; it has everything he needs. He further praises London when he declares, "O place! O people! Manners framed to please/All nations, customs, kindreds, languages!" The worldliness of London is thus addressed; it is a city for everyone, no matter where they are from.

The narrator feels he is entitled to the city's wealth of plenty because it is the "blest place of my nativity!" And, as a "free-born Roman," one who lives in the city of his birth, he feels entitled to every liberty it has to offer.

Donne's examination of the nature of commitment in his narrator's relationship is based first on sexual attraction for the person of his desire and then, after his desire's consummation, the mysterious nature of love itself.

In the terminology of the day, to "die" meant that one had experienced sexual gratification, a reference to "the little death" of the orgasm and the sleep that follows. In line 21, Donne's poet states that, "We're tapers too, and at our own cost die."

In other words, we are "candles" burning away, and eventually burning out is the price we pay for coming to life in the first place. There is a double meaning at work here, as the narrator must also be referring to either the sex act itself or acknowledgment that love does not last forever either.

By consummating a relationship through sex, "The phoenix riddle hath more wit/By us: we two being one, are it." That is, like the mythological phoenix who jumped into its own funeral pyre only to reemerge more powerful from its ashes, the act of sexual intercourse brings a couple together in unison where they become like one in the mysterious fire of love.

Herrick and Donne's narrators both recognize the fact that in death they Can/both commit themselves forever to their loves. Herrick's banished poet states, "For, rather than I'll to the West return,/I'll beg of thee first here to have mine urn." His ultimate happiness, then, is to be forever committed to the city of his love by having his ashes interred there.

Similarly, Donne's narrator recognizes that, in death, the love between he and his mistress will "live" forever when he says, "We can die by it, if not live by love." And while his love may die with him, it will be preserved forever for others to be inspired by because "it will be fit for verse" that others who come after will read.

And write about.

A WIT REVEALED

A wit is not a wit if he falls in love. A wit must always hide his true emotions, disguise them and never let them take control of him. To show emotion is to lose control of a given situation, something a wit must never do. However, as all people are susceptible at one point or another in their lives to the overriding demands of their emotions, so too is Sir George Etherege's wit Dorimant in his play *The Man of Mode*. Dorimant not only lets his emotions take control of him, he falls in love with Harriet, a woman of greater wit than himself.

It is the critical first scene in Act Four that pits these two wits against each other and provides the magic spark that ignites their love, establishing the tone of what looks to be a long-term relationship. The spark occurs between lines 99 and 168, in between which the conversation progresses from an examination of the implications of physical female appearances to a discussion of the nature of love.

The entire scene involving Dorimant and Harriet in Act Four comes across as a conflict of wit vs. wit, a figurative arm wrestling match in which the opponents push back and forth at each other until one finally breaks. This particular match appears to end with Harriet the victor; it is Dorimant who admits to himself his love for Harriet and in doing so betrays his wit to his emotions.

From line 99 to line 138 the two go back and forth discussing the nature of Harriet's physical appearance, the exchange of wit that sets up Dorimant's defeat. At first, Dorimant tries to sweet-talk Harriet by telling her, "You have a sweetness of your own, if you would but calm your frowns and let it settle" (IV.1. 108-109), to which Harriet replies, "My eyes are wild and wand'ring like my passions, and cannot yet be tied to rules of charming" (IV.1. 110-111).

From Harriet's reply, it would appear obvious that she will not give in to Dorimant's advances without resistance, if she will give in at all. Dorimant asks her to, "Put on a gentle smile and let me see how well it will become you"(IV.1.120-121), and a second time Harriet puts him off, replying, "I am sorry my face does not please you as it is, but I shall not be complaisant and change it" (IV.1.122-123).

Again, Dorimant is denied control over Harriet's actions; perhaps this resistance to domination causes Dorimant to fall in love with the girl. For, in resisting Dorimant's advances of wit, Harriet's own strength and independence are revealed, traits that are held in great importance by the wit. Harriet drives the final nail into the coffin of Dorimant's wit by saying, "Beauty runs as great a risk exposed at court as wit does on the stage, where the ugly and the foolish all are free to censure" (IV.1.137-138). Harriet includes both herself and Dorimant in this statement, implying that both her beauty and his wit are subject to sudden exposure, only to reveal the emotions that lie underneath. Beauty at the court becomes a superficial fact as the substance beneath the face is examined, just as the wit on stage is revealed to have true emotions behind his facade of wit.

Ironically, Dorimant is this "wit on stage," exposed to the audience by the manipulation of Etherege's pen through Harriet's comments. Just as Harriet states that the wit is subject to exposure, Dorimant is revealed to have fallen prey to his emotions, admitting that, "I love her and dare not let her know it" (IV.1.139).

Not only does Dorimant admit to himself (as well as to the audience) that he loves Harriet, he also admits that she may have revealed herself to be stronger than he, saying, "I fear sh'as an ascendant o'er me and may revenge the wrongs I have done her sex" (IV.1.139). In admitting his weakness, Dorimant at last succumbs to his emotions, leaving naught else but to let them take charge of the situation, which he chooses to do.

Dorimant now has no other option but to bring up the subject of love, which he accomplishes by stating, "Think of making a party, madam, love will engage" (IV. 1.141-12). Momentarily taken aback by Dorimant's admittance and having been stricken before with the "disease" of love, Harriet quickly recovers and continues to put Dorimant off, first warning him against falling in love, then stating that his talk of love will have little effect on her (lines 17-48 and 152-53). Dorimant responds that his advances of love have "been fatal" to which Harriet says, "To some easy women, but we are not all born to one destiny" (IV.1.157).

Harriet separates herself from other women, recognizing the fact that she is better than them (perhaps on account of her great wit) and that she is not the type to give in to her emotions without a very good reason, if at all. The scene ends with Dorimant not wanting to pledge his love for Harriet because of the presence of the other guests.

Harriet's response neither denies the fact that she will love him back nor affirms it, but leaves it up to Dorimant to pursue her interest. In telling Dorimant, "When your love's grown strong enough to make you bear being laughed at, I'll give you leave to trouble me with it" (IV.1.166-167). Harriet not only makes it clear that she will not reject his love for her, but also affirms that things between them will be on her terms.

By testing the strength of a wit's wit, this crucial scene reveals the inner nature of the wit, susceptible to emotion like anyone else. Just as beauty is superficial, so is wit. Beneath both lies the hidden truth, waiting to be revealed on the stage of life.

LOVE & HEARTBREAK

The death of love is the death of everything. The universe has no mercy. It shows you its dark side just when you think you are top of the world. You wander alone, thinking about your loves, thinking about your heartbreaks. Reality seems to slow to a standstill. The hours and nights are long and without laughter when life turns into a nameless thing you never imagined.

At some point, though, instinct kicks in (at least you better hope it kicks in) and despite your doubts, the cycle begins again. There is evidence of romance everywhere, a rubber band on the ground twisted into the shape of a heart, a kid standing on the corner singing, "what the world needs now is love, sweet love" while dangling a Styrofoam cup from a fishing pole, hoping for a handout.

The whole time you thought you had fallen into the void you were surrounded by your future. You just needed to welcome it and get on with your life. Romance isn't just hugs and kisses, it is a way to look at the world through crystal clear eyes. It is a way to acknowledge the epic nature of reality, a way of acting like it's Friday on a Monday night.

It is scars, fresh wounds, distant longings, nostalgia, regret, desire, and doubt, the whole spectrum of emotion that stems from our search for contact as we walk Planet Earth. We need to remind ourselves every now and then that creative collaboration is the source of all romantic fire.

Collaboration.

ANDREI TARKOVSKY'S STALKER:
AMUSEMENT PARK OF THE MIND

I like films that make me think. I like films that reflect life's uncertainties. I am comfortable with uncertainty in film because life is uncertain. That being said, I also love certain formula Hollywood films, especially when they are done well. There is something comforting about falling into the grip of a well-made fantasy.

Afterwards, though, I feel like I have compromised my mind, intelligence, and intellect, and I am left feeling manipulated. We *like* to be manipulated and yet, of all the things in the world there are to rebel against, manipulation is the first thing we should resist.

We want our lives to play out like formulaic Hollywood films, but the reality is that our lives play out more like Andrei Tarkovsky's *Stalker*. The first time I watched *Stalker* I was a freshman in college. I kept waiting for something to "happen." At the end of the movie, I thought, "that's it?" I was disappointed that we, the viewers, didn't get to go into The Room. Where was the resolution I was so used to from most of the movies I'd seen previously?

The second time I watched *Stalker* was twenty-five years later. A friend posted a clip from the film on her Facebook page. I was surprised by how contemporary and cool it looked. I rented it the next day and watched the first half, thinking of how film editing and pace have changed since the 70's when it didn't feel unnatural to sit through slow films that mirrored the slow pace of reality.

Tarkovsky had to shoot the film twice because there was a problem developing the film stock after the first shoot. Some of the locations where *Stalker* was filmed were contaminated with chemical toxins. Numerous people involved with the film, including Tarkovsky, died of cancer that, it was speculated, was caused by exposure to those chemicals. The thought that the making of a work of art may have led to its creators' demises is mind-boggling.

While watching the second half, I was surprised how much I had missed the first time. I was surprised by how many *ideas* the movie explored. Some of them make sense. Some of them are baffling. Some seem beyond comprehension.

Much, if not all of the film, is simply beautiful, more like a painting than a film. Its scenes unfold slowly, then something *seems* to happen, but is followed by...nothing? No.

Tarkovsky takes us along with his characters into The Zone and forces us to experience the place exactly as we would experience it for the first time if we were really there.

Revolution, not resolution, is what we should seek from art. It is the unfamiliar that pushes us towards new ideas by making us *think*. *Stalker* is just such a work of art, a wild and weird ride for the amusement park of the mind.

THREE: EXPERIENCE

ISABELLE EBERHARDT: OBLIVION SEEKER

"For the first time, I felt the savage intoxication of battle, bloody and primitive, of males body to body, wild with anger, blinded by fury, drunk on blood and instinctive cruelty. I knew the consuming voluptuousness of streaming blood, of the atrocious brutality of action triumphing over thought."

Sometimes it is music that frees the mind from its lethargy. Sometimes it is the mystical stupor of inebriation, and sometimes it is the hopeful euphoria that goes along with meeting new people. Sometimes these meetings take place on the page, in writing, where we discover the words of someone we can only know through the sum total of their publications.

The spirit of their ideas and the way they spent their time on Earth is often enough to make us feel as if we have discovered a kindred spirit, someone we would have liked to have known. Their words inspire us to take action against our own lethargy and attempt to live a life worth remembering, a life worth living. Isabelle Eberhardt is one of these people.

"To the one who understands the value and the delectable flavor or solitary freedom (for no one is free who is not alone) leaving is the bravest and finest act of all."

All good writing is travel writing, in a sense, because of the way it transports the mind from one place in the universe to another. And when a writer combines actual physical travel with the spiritual travel of a mind yearning for adventure and enlightenment the way Isabelle Eberhardt did, the results are mystical and able to inspire the reader to rebel against the common shape of his or her own life.

"His lust for life eased and he looked with disdain at the vanity of all violent efforts, of all devouring activities."

Raised by the anarchist Alexander Trophimousky in turn of the century Geneva, Eberhardt was aroused at an early age with the desire to travel and live in Africa. She wrote stories and travel essays based on the places she saw in Algeria, dressed as a man for her own protection as she rode horseback across the desert. She converted to Islam and was initiated into the secret Qadrya sect as a fellow mystic.

When an opportunity to fight against the French colonial forces in Africa reared its head, she threw herself into the fray alongside her Islamic friends. She drank, smoked kif, had numerous love affairs, and was the target of an assassination attempt by sword, carried out by either a rival sect who disapproved of her place in the Islamic religion, or by the colonial government, who viewed her as a threat to their influence over the local population. In 1904, two years after marrying an Algerian soldier, she was killed in a flash flood at the age of twenty-seven.

Championed early on by several admirers after her death, her diaries and writings survived through several generations until Paul Bowles translated *The Oblivion Seekers*, a collection of less than a hundred pages, in 1972.

It has only been in the last decade that much of her work has seen the light of publication, so that now the reader may discover her diaries, a novel, and four different collections of prose fiction and travel observations. And for those who would like to read a description of her life that, were it made into a movie, would rival Lawrence Of Arabia's epic scope, Annette Kobak's *Isabelle: The Life Of Isabelle Eberhardt* is an incredibly vivid and thoroughly cinematic reading experience.

"The vagrant longer for nothing. He hoped only for the limitless duration of that which existed."

Isabelle's writings are filled with the call of the open road, the melancholy of a wandering soul's search for home and a sense of place and wonder. Her diaries reveal a complicated and passionate person with an almost maniacal craving for experience and action. At the same time, she shows herself to be filled with the pensive melancholy of an introspective mind that felt constantly let down and unfulfilled.

These are the qualities that set the stage for a life of rebellion against the familiar roles that society at the time would have had her play. Like all true rebels, though, rebellion wasn't always on her mind. She was simply living the life that seemed to come naturally to her, a life in which identity had less to do with being defined and decided upon than it did with constantly being left open to redefinition, relocation, and reinvention.

"And Rei stopped, made breathless by the sudden revelation of the beauty of the earth and the fullness of life."

While a cult of Isabelle Eberhardt readers has grown steadily over the years, it seems an appropriate time for a reevaluation of her life and work to take place. It would be good to see her name alongside those of the infinite number of famous writers who have lived infinitely less inspiring lives.

Isabelle Eberhardt was one of those rare individuals who, throughout time, have rebelled against the perceived necessity to live a routine, "normal" life.

She inspires the reader to take to the road to view the world's infinite wonders and to fight against his or her lethargy with action.

FRANK STANFORD: CONSTANT STRANGER

"Really, I visualize the dead as well as the living. I visualize you who I will never know. We are constant strangers. I imagine you, I stare at you when I write."

When a writer dies, he or she dies two deaths and leaves two bodies behind, their physical body and their body of written work. It is the responsibility of the living to see that the writer's efforts to create a world on the page aren't wasted by allowing their words to slip and sink beneath the wake of passing time.

Frank Stanford is a writer whose work and legacy now sit dangerously close to the edge of oblivion. Of the eleven volumes of his work that were published both during his lifetime and after his death, only one, a collection of short fiction, *Conditions Uncertain & Likely To Pass Away*, is available today.

The rest of his books are out of print and hard to find, a fact that might lead some to believe that his work is neither important nor deserving of a larger audience and a proper evaluation by readers and critics alike.

Among poets and writers who have discovered Frank Stanford's work, though, just the opposite is true, as they have kept his writing alive by tracking down and Xeroxing for each other the rare volumes of his poetry that actually represent only a portion of the manuscripts he put together during his lifetime.

For many who stumble upon his words for the first time, there is a mixture of responses—inspiration at the scope and magnitude of his body of work; curiosity to know more about his life; and frustration with the fact that the thousands of pages of poems, stories, essays, and letters that make up his literary estate have, for the most part, languished in the twenty years that have passed since his death.

"If I was a pilgrim, I only had a raft and the river was low. If I was a poet, then who was Shelly and that one F. Villon. If I was trying to be somebody else, then why was I becoming myself."

Frank Stanford was born on August 1, 1948, in Mississippi. When he was twelve, he and his family moved to Arkansas. Three years later, after his father's death, he discovered that he was an orphan and had been adopted. He completed the last three years of his high school education in the Benedictine Academy in Subiaco, Arkansas, and was accepted into the University Of Arkansas Graduate Poetry Workshop in 1969. He left the program without fulfilling its degree requirements, spent many of his years as a self-described "traveling recluse," wrote extensively, and was married twice, the second time to the painter Ginny Stanford.

He was the subject of a documentary, *It Wasn't A Dream, It Was A Flood*, made in 1975 by his friend and first publisher, the writer and filmmaker Irv Broughton, whose Mill Mountain Press issued Stanford's first seven books of poetry.

He earned a modest living as a land surveyor, briefly ran a movie house that showed foreign films, and founded Lost Roads Publishers in an effort to bring to print the writers whose work he thought deserved to be read.

On June 3, 1978, he committed suicide by shooting himself three times in the heart with a twenty-two caliber pistol. He was twenty-nine years old.

"For some reason, danger calmed my nerves and made me sleep. As Jean Cocteau said, I think, the old myths are constantly being reborn without their heroes, their victims, knowing it, like lies who always tell the truth, the poet lives beyond his era, thus tragedy, therefore black comedy, ad infi..."

The manner of Frank Stanford's death left an indelible absence felt to this day by those who knew and loved him. A close reading of the body of work he left behind makes his passing seem even more poignant and senseless to those of us who can only know him through his writing. The twenty years since his death have seen the perpetuation of a Stanford "mystique" that, in some circles, has allowed his life and work to take on an almost mythic quality.

Caused, in equal parts, by a tendency of some critics to mistakenly point to his death as a way of understanding who he was and what his writing was all about, along with the steady disappearance and unavailability of his books, this "mystique" has disguised and overlooked the fact that, in his lifetime, he was an active participant in nearly every aspect of his chosen craft (writing, publishing, thinking about and speaking on his aesthetic ideas in interviews and correspondence with friends and other writers).

The Stanford "mystique" also does not acknowledge the fact that he did not die an unknown poet-- much of what he wrote, relative to the thousands of pages of writing he left behind, was published in chapbooks, books, and literary journals while he was alive by editors and publishers who recognized the beauty of his creative talent.

Much has been written about Frank Stanford the poet, yet he also wrote what amounts to several volumes of short fiction over the course of his life. He also did translations of poems by Vallejo, Bertolucci, Pasolini, Follain, and Parra, evidence that he recognized the need to champion the work of writers who would otherwise remain unpublished, neglected, and unread.

If one considers the fact that there exists today, in his literary estate and the private collections of those he knew and corresponded with, a reader's treasure trove of unpublished poems, stories, letters, essays, notes, and film scripts, it becomes obvious that Frank Stanford's legacy deserves to be championed by those who would like nothing more than to see his work back in print and available to the readers who have not heard of him yet.

"If we could think or dream, sending out a fleet of poems at the speed of light, or approaching the speed of light, what would we actually be doing. If a poem could travel the same distance light could in a year, then a poem I would launch now would be fifteen years old and passing thru this galaxy's edge and I would have been dead 45,000 years. There is something to all this and death."

Although much of the published criticism and analysis of Frank Stanford's work has been positive, some of it has wrongly suggested that his early death prevented him from finding his true writing voice and that, as a result, his work is undeveloped and immature. Nothing could be farther from the truth.

A close reading of his available writing--poetry, letters, fiction, and essays—reveals the presence of a confident, original voice and a personal aesthetic that was not only limited to literature, but also incorporated a deep understanding of painting, music, philosophy, and cinema. We can only speculate as to what might have come from Stanford's imagination had he survived the demons that led him to an early exit from this world.

In an essay titled "With The Approach Of The Oak The Axeman Quakes," Stanford wrote, "When the poet is young he tries to satisfy himself with many poems in one night. Later the poet spends many a night trying to satisfy the one poem. My poetry is no longer on a journey, it has arrived at its place."

One hopes that this statement might one day be fulfilled with a *Collected Works Of Frank Stanford* on the shelves of bookstores and in the hands of readers who might be moved or inspired by the words he left behind for us to read and carry with us as our own.

Note: Since this essay was first written, several previously unavailable and/or out of print collections of Frank Stanford's work have been published and/or returned to print.

FRANK STANFORD:
CONDITIONS UNCERTAIN
& LIKELY TO PASS AWAY

"I am reminded of the scene in the film by Cocteau where the fragments and shards of the broken mirror flow mysteriously back into themselves to form another mirror, another image."

Most, if not everything written about Frank Stanford's writing and life has been about his poetry and Frank Stanford the poet. When a *Collected Works Of Frank Stanford* is finally assembled one day, though, it will be more accurate to simply refer to him as Frank Stanford the writer because the truth of the matter is that he possessed an equal (and perhaps even greater) facility in the writing of unique and interesting fiction as he did in the creation of a huge body of interesting poetry.

This is not meant to in any way put down any of the thousands of poems he wrote, it is just to say that if he was a great poet, he was also a great fiction writer.

For the reader experiencing Frank Stanford's writing for the first time, *Conditions Uncertain & Likely To Pass Away*, a collection of eleven "tales," is a good place to start (in fact, the only place to start now that it is the only book of his still available and in print).

The stories in *Conditions Uncertain* are proof that Stanford was a writer who was able to bring poetic moments and images into his narrative writing as easily as he was able to bring a sense of story, character, and place to much of his poetry.

"A great man--but not as great as that Greek whose handwritten book I found--has said that all roads are long, and at the end of those roads what concerns us is how we walked them. This may be so for those who travel for the sake of travelling, but not for me. Oh yes, I've learned from walking, but it is what I find on the journeys that makes me step."

A character in one of the "tales," as Stanford called them, tells us that, "I plan to leave behind a book of essays dealing with the imagination." *Conditions Uncertain* is just such a book, for each of the stories in the collection, some just a few pages long, others approaching the length of short novellas, are filled with not just an interesting assortment of strange characters, narrators, and situations, but language and descriptions of the reality these characters inhabit that make a claim for the argument that the perception of the kaleidoscopic and hallucinatory nature of reality is also the most honest way of depicting it in writing.

In one of his letters, Stanford wrote: "I'm off my bearing, maybe, but you understand: you know what real is, so you don't have to describe what you don't understand as surreal (like others do)." These tales go beyond the realm of the surreal by weaving the twisting and bending webs of their narrator's stories with a chiaroscuro of dreams, nightmares, paintings, music, and stories within the tales themselves.

"His words were at once simple and complex. And he liked to drink and wander through the thickets of his past."

In "McQuiston's Tale," the narrator visits a blind man named Shing who claims to have a ventriloquist son with a dummy named Arimathea. Shing drinks a bottle of Tabasco and, even though he is blind, likes the color blue. In "DeMoss's Tale," the narrator is taken by Silent Night, the ice truck man, to have his hair cut by Rudy in the icehouse. He puts a frozen minnow in his pocket and goes to the carnival to see The Devil. "Hitchcock's Tale" is the horrifying account of what happens to a group of convicts being taken to prison in a wagon.

"Delainey's Tale" recounts a man's dream of a strange comedian who arrives in a boat called "The Setting" to inquire about some paintings. "Ansar's Tale & Luper's Note" is the story of an astronomer who goes blind and, while being taken care of by two young boys with an interest in the stars, remembers the stranger who arrived in his town when he was young and left books for him to read in his outhouse. "Merton's Tale" outdoes the strangest moments and people in a David Lynch film as a man, whose only possessions are a tape recorder and his collection of classical music, spends a few delirious nights stranded by a snowstorm in a strange town.

Stanford's characters are consumed by the weight of their dreams, memories, and experiences, and the reader isn't always sure if their perceptions of are the right ones to hold on to. As a result, Frank Stanford's stories are like those dreams we sometimes have that are filled with very strange people who we have never met, but who inhabit the world we often toss and turn through in our sleep.

His fiction reminds the reader that memories are as real as the experiences that shaped them and that dreams and nightmares are experiences that can help shape or bend our perceptions of the past and present.

With lines like "I felt the watch ticking against me all night like a grasshopper nailing a coffin," Stanford taps into a reservoir of surprising and jolting images and similes to create fictions that are at once disorienting and exhilarating to read. It is as if Stanford set out and successfully fulfilled one of his own character's statements: "I worked and worked the ore of my dreams until it was a fine radium."

The eleven tales in *Conditions Uncertain & Likely To Pass Away* represent only about a third of the short fiction that Stanford wrote in his lifetime. There are some twenty or so pieces of unpublished fiction in the Stanford estate—one hopes that they might made available sometime in the not too distant future, along with the rest of his unpublished and out of print work.

Only then will the true magnitude of Frank Stanford's artistic contributions be given a proper evaluation that will enable his future readers to see for themselves how his work frees the mind to better perceive reality's true strange shape.

FRANK STANFORD:
IT WASN'T A DREAM, IT WAS A FLOOD

In the essay "With The Approach Of The Oak The Axeman Quakes," Frank Stanford wrote: "I believe that the metaphorical imagination can be authenticated by the cinema." Friend and publisher Irv Broughton collaborated with Stanford to fulfill this belief with the making of *It Wasn't A Dream, It Was A Flood*, a twenty-six minute film described at the 1975 Northwest Film & Video Festival as "a dreamlike documentary about poet Frank Stanford filmed in Arkansas and Mississippi."

The film certainly is "dreamlike," its scenes and images reading like ingredients for a Stanford poem: mad laughter, a water wheel, a radio advertisement for an electric comb; mist hanging over a river, a nude man plowing a field, a giant moth crawling up the bark of a tree; a cemetery, the moon, cartoons, The Three Stooges, a young gypsy woman fortune teller; a soundtrack of classical music, funk, blues, and chirping crickets; a museum of relics, a chandelier made of toothbrushes, the pocket watches of monks who died, robed monks waiting on shore for another monk rowing towards them in a canoe with a black-draped coffin at the bow.

A second layer of the dream consists of people who knew Stanford talking about him. George Garrett: "He may see something the rest of us don't." A laughing Kenny Willette: "He's a crazy son of a bitch if you ask me… everything happens when Frank's around."

Assembled as a collage of still photographs and live-action sequences, it's the third layer where the film really "happens," as these scenes all belong to Stanford: napping on a porch, carrying what appears to be a wooden fish through the halls of the abbey, paddling a canoe, writing at a dining room table, laying in the sun on the shore of a river, walking down a dirt road wearing a white fedora.

Then there's the poet's voice, the film's most compelling element—hearing it for the first time, one realizes the depth of feeling behind his words on the page and senses the living presence of the man himself. Mostly he is heard in voiceover: talking about Greek mythology and its relationship to life in the South, the connection between the flow of life's imagery and ideas and their manifestation in poetry, the nature and qualities of monks, women, and especially dreams, the film's dominant theme.

Stanford asks, "I believe in dreams that come true. Do you?" He describes the monks as "dreamers and visionaries," and explains that he "put a lot of trust in dreams." Most memorable of all, Stanford reads his poem "Linger:"

I've fallen asleep
In the trees before
I dreamed someone's horse

Had wandered out on the football field
To graze
And I was showing children through a museum.

The film does feel like a museum of dreams with Stanford as its curator and guide taking the viewer on a tour of this parallel world.

In "The Axeman Quakes," Stanford wrote: "I was envisioning a film which still isn't finished, *Deathward*." The "film" of Frank Stanford's life and legacy is also still unfinished. One hopes that somewhere there is more footage of the poet and more recordings of his voice, because both help make real the spirit of a true visionary. As he wrote in a letter to poet Alan Dugan:

> If you were me, here alone, walking through the meadows and mountains, having a vision not too unlike the ones Whitman, Blake, and the singers in the Bible had, not thinking at all in terms of the literary world—but rather cells of inner worlds, almost audible in their movement— or of ever publishing all that you were sensing, would you undertake such a lengthly (sic) vision at this time in your life—if you were me?

Those who love his work need to undertake the completion of this vision on Stanford's behalf.

ATTILA JOZSEF: SHOCK THERAPY FOR THE NEW MILLENNIUM

"While I lived, I tried
  to stand up against the whirlwind."

Hungarian poet Attila Jozsef's eyes stare out from the cover of *Winter Night* with a look of tragic clarity, penetrating sadness, and what can only be described as some form of deranged contentment. Perhaps his short life (1904-1937) provides a clue to this look. He suffered through several nervous breakdowns and bouts of institutionalization and insulin shock therapy, then committed suicide at the age of thirty-two by throwing himself under a train. Yet despite the aura of melancholy that surrounds him, there are many hints of a sardonic sense of humor in Jozsef's work, such as this excerpt from his C.V.:

"I believe that my discovery of the tales of Attila the Hun had a decisive influence on all my ambitions ... this experience turned me into a thinking person, one who listens to the opinions of others, but examines them critically in his own mind; someone who resigns himself to being called "Steve" until one day he is justified in his belief that his name is Attila, as he had known all along."

With a clarity that acknowledges the extremes of feeling in the human mind, Jozsef's poems are shock therapy for the new millennium: angry, sad, hopeful, mystic, holy, epic, heroic, humble, disturbed—everything life is.

"Like fish and gods I survive
 in oceans and heaven alike."

SISTER CORITA KENT: COME ALIVE!

Certain individuals and their work, when discovered for the first time, appear to be familiar, as in *I think I've seen this before*. One has this feeling looking at a lot of art and writing that came out of the 1960s, and Sister Corita Kent's work is no exception: it features bright "psychedelic" colors, images of war, messages of protest, and cut and pasted texts mixed with advertising slogans to form statements about social issues.

We ascribe this sense of familiarity with a dismissive hand wave, without realizing that just because something appears to be "familiar" to us doesn't mean that it wasn't new, strange, and even revolutionary at some other point in time, and that it still might be so now if we are just able to look at it without preconceived ideas. It's in this way that the past becomes a great teacher, but only to the student who really wants to study, learn, and *see*.

Sister Corita Kent, like all true visionaries, was certainly about *seeing*. In Baylis Glascock's 1967 documentary *We Have No Art*, there is a scene in which Sister Corita tells her students that while watching films it is a good idea not to blink—that if one blinks one will miss something important.

Later in the film, she leads an audience through a "happening" of her own design: people in the audience are asked to turn around and place crepe paper hats on the people sitting behind them.

They are then asked to inflate a clear plastic glove and hold it to the other person's ear like they are telling them a secret while simultaneously reading an E.E. Cummings poem to their new neighbor and setting off poppers with confetti streams shooting out over the heads of the audience.

It is kind of a cliché 1960s moment, but then Sister Corita explains that each person in the scene is part of a larger whole; she was using the room and its occupants to paint a canvas whose totality only she was able to see from her vantage point at the podium. She describes the happenings that were part of the culture of the time as the breakdown between visual arts and theatre. In a similar fashion, Sister Corita invokes a phrase from the Balinese, who don't have a noun for the word "art" in their language: "We have no art. We do everything as well as we can."

She then explains that there is no distinction between art and "not art"; that the purpose of art is to give one an intense experience so that one might experience everything that is "not art" (life) more intensely; and that "a work of art is a small piece that you can digest which gives you a kind of idea of the richness that is in the whole."

Her book of teachings, *Learning By Heart: Teaching To Free The Creative Spirit* (co-created with Jan Steward) and the overview of her life and work *Come Alive! The Spirited Art Of Sister Corita* by Julie Ault are refreshing reminders that "our best times are when working and playing are the same" and that creativity is "the art of connection making." Sister Corita said *Learning By Heart* was "meant to be a workbook."

Divided into sections that explore the terms each chapter is named after and providing the reader with lessons and exercises to put those terms into action, Corita lays the groundwork for the reader to explore a variety of aspects of looking, sources, structure, making connections, tools and techniques, work and play, and what might have been Corita's most important theme: celebration.

This is a great book for artists, writers, and teachers and anyone who might be in search of a creative spark. Sister Corita states the obvious in ways one can apply to complex creative projects with an accumulation of phrases of wisdom supported by examples and exercises: "the goal is to get the greatest number of ideas"; "sources are starting points"; "the more tools and techniques you have, the broader will be your making vocabulary."

She playfully encourages one to "PLAY AT WORK: Take a few minutes during your lunch break to play with your office copy machine. You will immediately be able to see things in permutations that would otherwise take hours to imagine or achieve."

Julie Ault's book *Come Alive!* is a nuanced context for Sister Corita's life, work, legacy, and a colorful oversize journey through the images she created in her lifetime.

"With enthusiasm and a celebratory position on life, through her teaching and through her art," Ault writes, "Corita opened the way for various forms of liberation in the many individuals and institutions she affected over time. Heightened awareness, analytic consciousness, aesthetic innovation, political activism, collaborative spirit, collective experience, visual pleasure, intellectual empowerment, and serious fun are just a few of those forms."

Sister Corita said that the function of art is "to alert people to things they might have missed."

Her work, and these two books that capture the spirit and intent of her work, alert the reader to the existence of someone they might have missed until now, but whose lessons and words evoke a familiar and necessary presence.

HENRI CHARRIERE: BANCO

I've always considered tales of imaginative criminals and escapes to be inspirational, and have fond memories of some of the great films of my youth: *Butch Cassidy And The Sundance Kid*, *The Taking Of Pelham One, Two, Three*, and *The Great Escape*, among others. Possibly the greatest story of inspirational criminal literature belongs to Henri Charriere, a.k.a "Papillon," played by Steve McQueen in the movie of the same name. Sometime after seeing the movie I read the book, which left an indelible impression on me.

Recently I repeated the reading experience and was still amazed by Papillon's fourteen year-long tale of escape from the penal colonies of French Guiana after being sentenced to life for a murder he did not commit, where he spent almost a full three years of that time in solitary confinement. *Papillon*, still in print since its publication in 1968, is considered a classic, and rightfully so.

What a nice surprise it was, then, to discover that Charriere had also penned *Banco*, a sequel charting the course his life took *after* his great escape. Romance, escapades, heists, adventure, and more of Charriere's unique philosophical ruminations that made reading *Papillon* such a pleasure: *Banco* has them all. The book begins with Papillon wondering what to do with his newfound freedom: "I was just like a bird that, when you open the door of its cage, doesn't know how to fly anymore. It has to learn all over again."

Charriere ponders the task of going straight and finding a way to retire like some of the criminal friends he runs into early on in the book and decides that: "If the quiet life is too quiet, even though it's happy, it's not for me: that I know very well. Adventure! A man needs an adventure to feel alive, alive all through!"

We read inspirational literature to inspire us to set out on adventures of our own, however tame or criminal they might be, and this is reason enough to read Charriere's books. Few criminals (or non-criminals) have lived lives and written books that are equal in scope and as full of epic adventure. That he exhibits such a well-honed sense of honor, discipline, and relentless faith that he would succeed in achieving his liberation despite setbacks of a magnitude that would crush most people instantly is the real reason to join Papillon on his incredible flight.

ERNEST HEMINGWAY: ONLY A MAN

Three Hemingways emerged from my reading of the *Selected Letters* that seem the most critical for one to create an accurate appraisal of the writer's life. First there is Hemingway in Paris, where he began to practice the kind of writing he wanted to write. Second, the Hemingway in Cuba, living at the Finca Vigia from 1950-51, where he seemed to be at the height of his fame before the total acclaim that came following *The Old Man And The Sea*. The letters of this period are rich with detail, insight, and remembering along with hints of loneliness, sorrow, and a desire to distinguish between the "real" Hemingway and the public Hemingway. And finally, there is Hemingway in Ketchum, where he closes the circle of his writing life by working on *A Moveable Feast*, the memoir of his years in Paris, before committing suicide in 1961. It is interesting to observe Hemingway's writing style emerge, grow, and mature through the course of his letters, so that by the time he had published several successful books, his letters were as prosaic and poetic as his fiction.

In the midst of an excited letter from Boyne City, Michigan, there is a juxtaposition of Hemingway's still youthful and unrealized writing style with that of the emerging, future prose poetry that would fill his stories. At one point in the letter to Grace Quinlan, he exclaims, "Gosh G, what a hiker you are. 11 and 15 of the miles! That's real honest to God hiking. You must be having a peerless time." In the same letter, he writes about the attractive nature of travel flavored with hints of his emerging prose style:

"But then—it's all in the lap of the Gods. I'm for a job in New York next winter. But then I'm also for the open road and the long sea swells, and an old tramp steamer hull down on the oily seas. And waking up in the morning in strange ports. With new delightful smells and a tongue you don't understand. And the rattle of shifting cargo in the hold. And tall glasses and siphons and rare new stories and old pals in far places. And hot nights on deck with only pyjamas on. And cold nights when the wind roars outside and the waves smash against the thick glass of the port holes and you walk on deck in the flying scuds and have to shout to make yourself heard. And laying chin down on the grass on a cliff and looking out over the sea. And oh such a lot of things, G." (p. 37).

The letters of the Paris years have a different tone than the style Hemingway used later to write *A Moveable Feast*. They are full of excitement and giddy energy and there never seems to be a moment where he doubts his ability to survive in Paris. Everything seems easy and charmed. Just two days after arriving, he has marked out a routine and a place to work:

"Well here we are. And we sit outside the Dome Café, opposite the Rotonde that's being redecorated, warmed up against one of those charcoal brazziers and it's so damned cold outside and the brazier makes it so warm and we drink rum punch, hot, and the rum enters into us like the Holy Spirit" (p. 59).

There is no evidence here of the sorrow and nostalgic longing that will later define the tone of *A Moveable Feast*. One wonders what Hemingway would have thought while working on the book in Ketchum if he had been able to read this passage from a letter to William Horne, 17-18 July 1923, from Paris:

"We can't ever go back to old things or try and get the 'old kick' out of something or find things the way we remembered them. We have them as we remember them and they are fine and wonderful and we have to go on and have other things because the old things are nowhere except in our minds now" (p. 85).

Hemingway's Finca Vigia letters lead him towards reflection about the past and meditations on his real self compared to the version put forth in magazine articles, several biographies, and stories circulated in the gossip mill. Much of this period of his correspondence reads like a self-defense of Ernest Hemingway, as if he were a heavyweight boxer obsessed with his skills in addition to how the public viewed those skills and the man behind the punches. An excerpt from a letter written in 1950 is a good example:

"In night clubs people will come up to you and say 'So you're Hemingway are you?' and swing on you without further explanation. Or they will paw you, which a man doesn't like or start to paw your wife or some girl you know, and if you admonish them, warn them, and then have to clip them, it gets in the papers" (p. 709).

Hemingway is no longer the anonymous young writer able to work unbothered in a café in Paris, but someone who has sought refuge on an island to be as far away as possible from intrusion and who finds himself feeling lonely there:

"Lately I am lonely quite a lot, not having the children around and not liking the way things go so that picking up the paper is like (we'll skip it). Anyway I write letters because it is fun to get letters back. But not for posterity" (p. 695).

Other times he seems to be want to hold onto who he really is without being reduced to the clichés that his public persona are defined by:

"It is never in the papers that you wake at first light and start working; nor that you serve your country in any way you have ever been asked to; nor that you, your brother and your eldest son were all wounded and decorated in the last one, nor that your two grandfathers both fought and were wounded in the Civil War, nor that you were wounded on 22 different occasions and have been shot through both feet, both legs, both thighs, both hands and had six bad head wounds due to enemy action. Nor that all the ambition you ever had to be the best American prose writer and to work at it hard and not foul anybody" (p. 709).

The contradictions between his public and private selves seem to come to a head for Hemingway in 1951, when he complains to Arthur Mizener:

"You know it is a horrible thing to be somebody's hero and have them attribute all sorts of qualities to you when you are only a man trying to work at it as well as you can" (p. 717).

That same year Hemingway exudes a feeling of accomplishment and of having concluded a long ascent after writing *The Old Man And The Sea*:

"This is the prose that I have been working for all my life that should read easily and simply and seem short and yet have all the dimensions of the visible world and the world of a man's spirit. It is as good prose as I can write as of now" (p. 738).

Ten years later in Ketchum, Hemingway appears unable to write a full, "true" sentence, resorting to clipped, unsteady prose that resembles a telegram in this letter to L.H. Brague, one of his last:

"Try to only think from day to day and work the same but things have been rough and are rough all over. Cuba situation—lack of library to work from—etc. Will not bitch on but thought you would like a situation report. Certainly hope this girl Mary took the MSS to can read my handwriting. Had to copy all corrections on pages in large school boy hand. This is all being done under difficulty but it is being done" (p. 918).

Hemingway's letters reveal more about his writing and life than any biography written about him. All the nuances and contradictions of the various phases of his life are contained in them for the reader willing to take the time to assemble the puzzle they represent. In the end, they will discover what Hemingway knew all along despite his acclaim, that he was only a man.

SAUL WILLIAMS:
"CODED LANGUAGE" DECODED

A key line in Saul Williams' call to action, art and activity in his poem "Coded Language" arrives about halfway through: "Your current frequencies of understanding outweigh that which has been given for you to understand."

Williams is acknowledging and bringing to light what we all know to be true but fail to follow up with tangible activity, that what we *sense* reality could be far outweighs the reality we live, that what we *sense* we know far outweighs what we are told to be "true," and that our imaginations, so fine-tuned to believing anything is possible from years of exposure to special effects and alternate realities, are beginning to sense a greater reality than the fictions that have invaded our minds.

We sense this when we find ourselves listening to music and hypnotized in a way leads us to feel a heightened sense of awareness. In moments like these, we rise up above the mundane state of everyday reality.

The next day at the job or school isn't as hypnotic and euphoric. Time slows and drags. Saul Williams' poem is a call to action for all of us to reverse this trend of lethargy in reality by making art, by creating.

The idea is not to think of creativity as a living, as a means to an end, nor in terms of failure or success, but as an act that unites us.

Williams' lays down the course of the recent revolution in consciousness that has taken place at the hands of the DJ with the idea that the incorporation of the entire range of human musical history into music in the form of samples and loops has united the past with the present and, as a result, created a new future that we are in the process of figuring out.

Williams refers to the beat, the fundamental rhythm that makes us move, as a force for positive change. He states that listening must be turned up a notch to overcome the aggressors of language? Who might he be referring to? Politicians? Mainstream media?

This poem attacks the status quo, the way things are, and challenges the reader and listener to embrace and act out what they really know.

"Reject mediocrity," Williams instructs. Television will not do this for you, but creating your own art will.

Williams' invokes the names of his literary, musical, and political ancestors before laying down his manifesto for the future, a declaration that each of us should embrace if we want to see things change and if we want reality to equal what our imaginations tell us is possible.

When you read this poem, will you breeze over Williams' list of names or will you take the time to look them up and learn about the work they have done?

The future, if it is to be changed and actively evolved into something that better resembles what we want it to be, requires some effort. Have you done anything today to achieve this goal?

Music releases us. Art invigorates. Saul Williams is asking you to produce, not simply consume. He is asking you to reverse the flow of consumption: video store, DVDs, downloading, listening, movies, video games, TV shows...

Instead, substitute with painting, playing an instrument, making a movie, writing a poem, and uploading these things to inspire and influence others who might be ready to take the next step themselves.

Decode all coded language. Exist.

SYLVIA PLATH:
"THE ARRIVAL OF THE BEE BOX"

In "The Arrival Of The Bee Box," the poet/narrator's bee box becomes not only the owner's property and responsibility, but also an image symbolic of life and death, the power of which the narrator holds in her hands. The poem's movement is from death out into life. In the first stanza, the "clean wood box" appears to the narrator as "the coffin of a midget/or a square baby." The image of the baby suggests the pregnancy that the bee box also represents. "I have to live with it overnight," the narrator muses, "And I can't keep away from it."

In the morning, when she "will set them free," the bees will no longer be entirely controlled by her, as anything that is born or created, child or poem, is no longer entirely in the hands of its creator. It is the process of creation within the poem that moves the narrator's thoughts from death towards life. "There are no windows, so I can't see what is in there," she says. The third stanza underscores the image of a dark place from which something mysterious will emerge to create something beautiful: "It is dark, dark," "black on black."

"How can I let them out?" the narrator asks, as if speaking both about the bees and the poem about the bees, or any poem that might emerge from "the noise," "the unintelligible syllables." From this din, honey comes.

The last stanza of the poem depicts the poet/narrator "in my moon suit and funeral veil." "I am no source of honey," she says, "So why should they turn on me?" Here the narrator's tone is that of someone tainted by death: "no source of honey." But, setting the bees free, she will be "sweet God." The last line, "the box is only temporary," uses the word *temporary* to underscore the poem's motion from coffin to the bee's release and creation of honey.

The word also seems to refer to the narrator's state of mind: images of creation played against images of death; poems and honey from the dark dins, all temporary.

ELIZABETH BISHOP:
"QUESTIONS OF TRAVEL"

In "Questions Of Travel," Elizabeth Bishop's narrator ponders the value of travelling to a place far from home "to be watching strangers in a play in this strangest of theatres." The poem suggests the awareness that can be jarred into being when one leaves home and, because it is a poem of questions, the reader is left in the position to decide for him or herself if it is better to "have stayed at home, wherever that may be." The movement and language of the poem are like the streams and waterfalls alluded to in the first stanza. The narrator's stream of thought moves through descriptions of actual streams to a two hour rain that leads the traveller to write her questions of travel in a notebook.

The first stanza uses images of speed and irreversible movement to underscore the passage of time. Crowded streams hurry too rapidly down to the sea, and if they aren't waterfalls yet, "in a quick age or so, as ages go here, they probably will be." Bishop then uses the image of "the hulls of capsized ships" to emphasize the end of time's travel into the future, where death approaches, "slime-hung and barnacled."

The second section of the poem raises questions of the value of and absurdity of escaping one's surroundings and present moment for another moment in another place.

Travelling to another place leads the narrator to ask, "Where should we be today?" Images of "home" are contrasted against images of strangers, the tiniest green hummingbird, some inexplicable old stonework, and "one more folded sunset," views "instantly seen and always, always delightful," but still far from home, where maybe the traveller should have stayed.

The final section of the poem before the traveller/narrator raises her questions of travel uses a list to create the contrasting sensations of the value of things seen on a trip versus their actual significance.

Mundane things seen in another country become "really exaggerated in their beauty," yet "surely it would have been a pity" not to have seen them. Bishop uses images of trees along a road, the sound of wooden clogs on a grease-stained filling station floor, a fat brown bird in a bamboo cage.

The thoughts of history these things lead to mean that the value of the narrator's journey, wherever he or she has gone, is decided not by the actual place or things seen, but by the thoughts and questions they inspire.

PHILIP LEVINE:
"I SING THE BODY ELECTRIC"

I found solace in Philip Levine's poem "I Sing The Body Electric." "People sit numbly at the counter waiting for breakfast or service," Levine writes, and there I was, in the Newman Center, in Reddy's Restaurant, in the Whately Diner, hiding behind my menu, looking around the room for poetry, for poets, for people who might write poetry, for people who might read poetry, but with no luck.

"I have come in out of the cold and wind of a Sunday morning of early March," Levine writes, "and I seem to be crying, but I'm only freezing and unpeeled." *Only* freezing? *Only* unpeeled?

The waitress brings coffee in a cracked cup. The coffee spills all over the narrator's newspaper, in which it is written that poetry is dying, "In Iowa, Missoula, on the outskirts of Reno, in the shopping galleries of Houston." Poetry is dying? Poetry is dead?

I found solace in this poem because it was a confirmation that poetry is alive, everywhere, and in everyone: "Men keep coming in and going out, and two of them recall the great dirty fights between Willy Pep and Sandy Sadler, between little white perfection and death in plaid trunks."

The lonely, melancholy, or merely detached poet wants to tell these men that he saw these fights, but the story of taking the train smelling of vomit and piss is a legend "better left to die."

The tone of this poem made me wonder what the poet expects from being a poet. He has crossed a continent to bring these citizens the poems of the snowy mountains.

Like Walt Whitman, Levine sings the song of himself. In this poem, though, his spirit is seemingly disillusioned. Or is it?

"Nothing is alive in this tunnel of winds of the end of winter except the last raging of winter," he writes. Dark clouds are "lined only with smaller dark clouds."

Or poems.

ADRIENNE RICH: "DARKLIGHT"

Adrienne Rich uses color and light in her poem "Darklight" to create an impressionistic painting/poem that evokes the quality of "the ancient hour/between light and dark, work and rest/ earthly tracks and star-trails."

Part 1 of the poem begins with the greys and blues of dawn giving way to "An eye, coming in closer." Each of the three segments of Part I of "Darklight" create the image of an eye poking through the morning fog. In the second verse, it is the "thrown husk of a moon/sharpening in the last dark blue" which leads the poet/narrator to "think of your eye."

The way Rich structures this poem is the way memory works on itself in the first light of day and the last dark of night. The eye of the person that appears is like the sun, "coming in closer," taking over the day with a huge "tear that washes out the eye,/The tear that clears the eye."

The "Darklight," then, leads to clear-sight, a way of seeing and thinking totally detached from the rational way of seeing and thinking that the day demands, yet at the same time comfortable with crystal abstractions: the grey light, the blue sky, the fog, the husk of a moon, the last dark blue, the eye that makes "dark the light/that washes into a deeper dark," the eye of a remembered lover, a forgotten person, a stranger who might have once looked the poet's way, leading her to write a poem of the ancient hour, between reason and the unconscious, "the last willed act of the day/and the night's first dream," an eye, my eye, your eye.

CHARLES WRIGHT: "SOUTHERN CROSS"

"I can't remember enough," Charles Wright writes in his book and poem of the same name *The Southern Cross*. "I'll never be able to." But what Wright does remember, as in the poem "Gate City Breakdown," are the details that bring into existence moments, memories, impressions, feelings, "the dust we leave," so that in the end it is easy to forget the poet's faults, "so ridiculous, and full of self-love," and easy to "remember me once/Slide-wheeling around the curves,/letting it out on the other side of the line."

Wright is reminding us to remember the things that are worth remembering because, as he writes in "Self-Portrait," "This world is a little place,/Just red in the sky before the sun rises./Hold hands, hold hands/That when the birds start, none of us is missing."

"The spirits are everywhere," Wright says in "Ars Poetica," and wherever he is, nothing can help the poet forget or ignore "The voices rising out of the ground,/The fallen star my blood feeds,/this business I waste my heart on."

The business of poetry, for Wright, is the search for spirits in things and places and memories, the spirits of people gone, lost, remembered. It is the business of creating a place to feel alive, as if poetry is able to grant freedom, if only temporary, from the spirits that haunt us. As if, by remembering these things, by writing them down, we can...what?

"What will it satisfy?" Our need to remember, if not everything, some of it, and to never forget "the past,/with its good looks and Anytime, Anywhere..."

IGNAZIO SILONE: BREAD AND WINE

About halfway through Ignazio Silone's novel *Bread And Wine*, Pietro Spina, disguised as a priest, asks another priest, Don Luigi, "What would happen if men remained loyal to the ideas of their youth?" "The time always comes," he said, "When the young find that the bread and wine of their home have lost their flavor and they look elsewhere for their nourishment. Only the bread and wine of the tavern at the crossroads of the great highways can assuage their hunger and their thirst. But man cannot spend all his life in taverns." This is perhaps the most telling moment in the story, revealing the difference between those who choose to live out their ideals and those who choose the other, more inevitable path of giving in to an ordered existence. For both kinds of people there are consequences, but for those who choose to live out the ideals of their youth, the consequences might be to inspire others to live their lives in a different way, more true to their ideals. At the same time, the consequences of living out one's youthful ideals, especially in the realm of politics, can be grave. Don Paolo knows this.

He has not returned to his native soil simply to recuperate, but also to regain a sense of what turned him into a revolutionary to begin with. Early on in the book, in Chapter Eight, he expresses the disdain of one who sees too much, who has achieved a state of too much knowledge, and who wishes he could return to a simpler, naive state:

"If only I could go to sleep and wake up, not just with healthy lungs, but with the brain of an ordinary man, free of all abstractions. If only I could go back to ordinary, real life. Digging, ploughing, sowing, reaping, earning a living and talking to the other men on Sundays. Obeying the law that says: Thou shalt earn thy daily bread in the sweat of thy brow. When I come to think of it, perhaps the real cause of my distress is my defiance of the ancient law...."

Here, in this moment of doubt and remorse about who he has become, the revolutionary questions his chosen path, but later realizes that "the cause of my pain is the question whether I have been faithful to my promise."

At a certain point, the forces that be clash with the revolutionary who seeks to change those forces and his path becomes not so much a chosen one as an inevitable road down which he must travel, no longer concerned with his own safety, but with how his actions will be perceived by those who come after him. Don Paolo comes into contact with Murica, a young, like-minded man, and it is at this point that we see that the priesthood and the path of the revolutionary are the same in that they are both about passing on faith from one generation to the next. "There are infinite gradations of consciousness," Don Paolo says, "Just as there are of light."

RALPH ELLISON: INVISIBLE MAN

Ralph Ellison's *Invisible Man* moves in and out of light and darkness, as its main character moves from blind sleep to illuminated awareness. The novel opens with the narrator "hibernating" underground. Hibernation, to him, is a "covert preparation for a more overt action."

He has wired his ceiling with 1,369 lights and plans to wire the walls and eventually even the floor of his underground room with light, because, as he states, "Nothing, storm or flood, must get in the way of our need for light and ever more and brighter light. The truth is the light and light is truth."

Throughout the early fourth of the book, the narrator is repeatedly subjected to situations that shock his way of thinking and lead him to the next level of awareness, where he finds himself less blind and more illuminated about the way things are in his world.

His initiation begins with the Battle Royal, in which he and several other black men are blindfolded and made to fight with each other in a boxing ring while rich, drunk white businessmen and townspeople watch.

When the narrator sees a naked white woman dancing in the ring for the entertainment of the businessmen, he is strongly attracted and continues to look when some of the other black men are looking at the ground. "Had the price of looking been blindness, I would have looked," he writes.

For the rest of the novel, the narrator follows a similar course of action of looking and finding himself shocked and awakened by what he sees, and hears. Smoking reefer and listening to music in the opening chapter leads the narrator to "a new analytical way of listening to music," in which "the unheard sounds came through." He is able to hear "the silence of sound" and later, we can see his situation through this method of listening.

The narrator becomes invisible when he realizes that no one can see or hear him because they are sleepwalking through life, far removed from the illuminated state of "wakeful living." At the end of the novel, the narrator declares, "the hibernation is over. I must shake off the old skin and come up for breath." If he fulfills this promise and emerges from his underground existence to fulfill a "socially responsible" role, his appearance will be in an open doorway with the blinding glare of thousands of lights behind him as he leaves his basement room bathed in the illumination of self-awareness.

His awakening began in blindness, led to the shocks of initial awareness, and drove him into an underground existence filled with light, where he discovered that it is possible for the "unheard sounds" to come through.

That the narrator leaves us without a clue about what will happen next is a challenge, as if he is saying, "here is the light, what do *you* see with it?"

HENRY JAMES: THE AMBASSADORS

The Ambassadors is about the awakening, or reawakening, of one man's imagination. Strether's imagination is restored when he travels to Paris and begins to understand "the values." Strether is sent abroad on a mission to rescue Chad Newsome from the grip of what his family in New England perceives to be some kind of evil, but when Strether finds the young Chad to have been vastly improved by his time in Paris, and when he finds Chad's new lady friend to be a woman of exquisite grace and breeding instead of the harlot his family thought he would find, he is forced to reevaluate and reshape his role as "ambassador." Paris has not only changed Chad Newsome, it also changes Strether by reminding him of the sensations of his own youth and by re-invigorating his own soul with some of those feelings.

"Poor Strether had at this very moment to recognize," James writes in Book Second (II), "the truth that wherever one paused in Paris the imagination reacted before one could stop it. This perpetual reaction put a price, if one would, on pause; but it piled up consequences till there was scarce room to pick one's steps among them." Strether recognizes his own missed life, but during the course of his trip to Paris he sees the chance for Chad to prevail by avoiding the same mistake. "Don't neglect your opportunities to live," Strether tells Chad. "You have only one life...live it to the full. If you haven't had that, what have you had?"

Strether is a changed man by the end of the novel, though he realizes it is too late for him to change his life. The important thing is that a change does take place and that he emerges from his journey with new eyes, or at least eyes with their metaphorical cataracts removed.

I could not help but read this novel in light of my own travels through Paris and the moods and experiences I have gone through as a result of being there. I have walked, like Strether, the Paris streets. I have looked and listened and taken note of things seen and heard. I have waited for a woman in a cafe near the Seine, and after I said goodbye to her a few days later near the Louvre at the top of the stairs leading down to her metro, I turned and walked through an unpopulated traveling carnival, past the riderless carousel, past the museum, and next to the Seine. Although I was miserable about saying goodbye and not knowing when I would see her again, I recognized that at least I was miserable in Paris and walked back to the hotel with this thought in mind.

I have been to many other cities in the world, but Paris casts a spell that does not dissipate, but rings and echoes and expands until a part of you has been changed forever. Strether and Henry James know this feeling well.

HAVE YOU FOUND THE JOY?

There's a hostel on Broadway not far from where I live. Sometimes I see travelers emerge from the hostel's alley entrance next to the piroshky shop and look up and down the street. I like to imagine that this is their first look at everyday life in Seattle, that piroshky is their first taste of "Seattle Cuisine," and that Broadway, the street of dreams, beckons them to explore, to wander, to look around.

I try to remember my own first glimpse of Broadway: it was night and my friends had taken me to several bars before heading back to their apartment. I stood on the corner in front of Ileen's. I looked left. I looked right. Broadway seemed to go on forever in each direction. I wondered what would happen to me in Seattle, I wondered who I would meet. Was anyone waiting to meet me? The night pulsed and glimmered with psychedelic possibility.

Now, years later, there are some days when I have to remind myself that everything is new, that everything is still possible, that just because I am late for work doesn't mean I won't soon be able to take a long and leisurely lunch with the newspaper in hand and the world wandering by. There are stories happening every day, all around.

Last week I saw a sparrow and a pigeon sitting next to each other on a telephone wire. The squirrel who lives nearby took a sun nap on top of the fence outside my window last week and this morning arrived to ask for a handout. I gave him a piece of bread and watched as he sat and ate it on the fence while I ate my own breakfast standing at the kitchen counter. My friend from the neighborhood, Mr. Squirrel.

A kid on Broadway, sitting on top of a newspaper vending machine, reported to a blind man walking by that it was a beautiful day, that the sun was shining, and the sky was blue. An angry man in front of the video store ground his lit cigarette into the mouthpiece of a payphone and announced to everyone within hearing range that "the cops are monitoring this goddamn phone!"

A confused woman at the post office walked up to me with a letter in hand and said, as if it was her first time: "Where do I mail these?" I pointed to the mailbox that was just a foot or two away. "Oh, thank you." she said, "I'm new here in town."

All these little pieces, fragments, details within the main narrative of job, routine, friends, music, parties, bills, attempted creative endeavors, they all begin to add up to a whole that reminds me I am still and always will be a tourist, even after all my decades on Planet Earth.

I met a friend for a beer last night. Over a pitcher of Hefeweizen she told me about her time in India doing volunteer work at a home for the dying. She showed me pictures of some of the people she encountered in her daily life in Calcutta and told me stories about each of them: the man whose job was giving shaves to men on the street, the sign painter, the curry maker, the ice deliverer. She told me about meeting Mother Theresa, who leaned forward to inquire about her experience so far in India. "Have you found the joy?" she asked.

Have you found the joy?

TWELVE TONS OF CHICKEN

As I write this, Hurricane Katrina is battering the South, with much of the population being referred to as "refugees," with some camped out in the Superdome and hundreds of thousands taking to the road for higher ground.

A little nod should go out to all those who aren't going to be able to eat in the normal relaxed style they are accustomed to for days, if not weeks, many of whom might not have kitchens to return to.

In recent food news, a woman's winning recipe earned her a prize of 12 tons of pre-cooked chicken. Scientists analyzing data from the Mars Rover Spirit have discovered some puzzling features: blueberries, cobbles, and rinds. "Once we nail the cobbles problem, we may go after the rinds next," one scientist said.

"Sadaam Hussein prefers Raisin Bran Crunch to Fruit Loops and his favorite snack was Cheetos until he discovered Doritos corn chips." "British balloonist David Hempleman-Adams hosted "the world's highest formal dinner party" at 24, 262 feet (asparagus, salmon, and terrine of summer fruits)."

"On the space shuttle Discovery, Japanese astronaut Soichi Noguchi dined on "Space Ram," a new zero-gravity instant noodle invented by Momofuku Ando, who invented the instant noodle in 1958." "The popsicle celebrated its 100th anniversary."

"Sonya Thomas, a.k.a. "The Black Widow" on the competitive eating circuit, ate 35 brats in 10 minutes to win the Johnsonville Brat-Eating World Championship. The previous record was 19.5 brats in 10 minutes." "450 sheep jumped to their death off a cliff in Turkey as their shepherds watched helplessly. A total of 2000 sheep jumped; those who survived were cushioned by the "billowy white pile" at the bottom of the cliff."

"Gerry Thomas, the "inventor of the TV dinner," died; it was later reported that this was a tall tale and though he worked at Swanson, he had little to do with the product." "In a New Mexico prison, prisoners who throw their food are fed Prison Loaf, an entire meal ground up, floured, and baked. One jail employee said "It wasn't that bad, it kind of tasted like a carrot loaf with fish in it.""

"100 monkeys in Bangladesh refused to eat food for several days as they mourned the murder by a young man of one of their group." "Mexico's centuries-old tradition of eating bugs has become more lucrative." "A man who swims nude in Sausalito has shocked diners and prompted complaints to police."

And in Niger, a family of six dines on a single rat, the only food they'd had for a week in the famine-stricken nation where, the news reporter said: "even the rats are starving." Which raises the simple and obvious question: why is there so much hunger in the world when there is so much to eat?

Bon appetit.

AFTERWORD: THE SHAMAN

All forms of experience are electrical in nature. Things that charge us with energy are filled with energy. By "electrically-charged" we do not mean the force of a current as caused by electrical impulses, but the force of energy raised high enough to stimulate our curiosity and make us consider the possibility of higher levels of reality.

By "reality" we mean wherever you are and whatever you are doing. Regardless of your location in time and space there is always a higher level of awareness available to you if you are able to walk through the doors that lead to them.

Certain events are filled with the kind of electricity that jolts us into awareness. We know we are alive when we are aware of the higher planes of reality at work parallel to our own.

It is easy to take no action. It is just as easy to act. You see a face you want to know. You must talk to him or her. You must act. If his or her eyes look back at yours, it is possible they are a seeker too.

People look but do not act. Or, they act without looking. Fear is the wall that must be broken down. If you want to know someone, there is only one course of action. Ignore the flood of fear and doubt. In the end, you will wish you had gotten to know more of the faces you once saw and wanted to meet but never saw again.

Willingness to act.

In seeking, you must be ready to find. You must make yourself available to all forms of experience. The seeker is always seeking. There is no end to his or her search, though he or she may long for an end to the endless state of looking. The seeker knows that seeking and finding are constant states of travelling and arriving, but is there one single destination for the seeker, one face or place where he or she "belongs?"

All journeys are finite until we enter the age of mass space travel. We are stuck on the face of planet Earth, but on this finite globe exist infinities to seek and find. The seeker seeks another who is also limitless. He or she looks into the eyes of everyone he or she sees. Some eyes suggest the limitlessness of vast possibility, but mask a morbid finiteness, an inward-spiraling gyre of lethargy. The seeker must never be convinced of another's limitlessness when it does not exist.

The seeker reflects the light of the world. He or she is the lens and the screen, the music and the instrument, the shadow of the light that illuminates the corners of the Earth. The journey has no end. The stars in the sky will live and die but the seeker lives forever, moving from one age to another, spreading the curious fire, forcing the eyes to open and swallow and blink at the sight of all that is within sight.

An accumulation of words is no substitute for experiences. You may never see the face again that looked familiar and struck a chord you recognized. Learn to negate the forces of sabotaging interference. Thoughts of the unmet nags at the minds of the two who wanted to meet but didn't.

The nag of what will never be.

There is urgency to our existence. It should remind us to act on our desires and creative impulses. One day we will be no more. Today, we are.

The most obvious forms of electrical experience are fate and coincidence. By their seemingly random nature, fate and coincidence reveal to us that there are invisible forces at work, and that while these forces are invisible, they are not unfelt.

We sense these forces when we are in the midst of their spell, and sometimes by sensing their manifestation we are able to utilize them to our advantage. One must make oneself open to the doors of fate and coincidence when they arrive. Their portals gesture for us to step inside and enjoy the mechanisms of their strange universe. A force is at work somewhere, sending us its greeting, cracking open the door of possibility and welcoming us inside.

135

Repeated experience with chance and coincidence prove that we are conductors of some kind of electrical force field that *makes things happen*. When we are gifted with the ability to see and welcome fate and coincidence into our lives, we are able to elevate ourselves above mindless, thoughtless rote. That which makes us think proves we exist.

It is for this that we must strive, it is for this that we must offer our minds to the hidden powers: once we have stepped into the realm of possibility, our imaginations know no end to what they can accomplish. Our movement towards what we desire will be accelerated and the invisible realm will become visible. From this plateau of new sight we will be able to imagine the peaks beyond. We must learn to see with new eyes. We must learn to *see*.

And then you meet; you are in each other's arms; he or she wants you as much as you want him or her. Sebadoh's "Brand New Love" plays here. The reader now listens to the song and the rest of *Sebadoh vs. Helmet* before proceeding.

"Shamans are peripheral to society's goings on in ordinary social life in every sense of the word. They are called on in crisis, and the crisis can be someone dying or ill, a psychological difficulty, a marital quarrel, a theft, or weather that needs to be predicted.

Among aspiring shamans there must be some sign of inner strength or a hypersensitivity to trance states.

One cannot be heard. The more one is able to articulate what it is, the less others are able to understand. This is why I think people who attain enlightenment, if we may for a moment co-map these two things, are silent. They are silent because we cannot understand them."

--Terence McKenna, "Tryptamine Hallucinogens And Consciousness," collected in *The Archaic Revival: Speculations On Psychedelic Mushrooms, The Amazon, Virtual Reality, UFOs, Evolution, Shamanism, The Rebirth Of The Goddess, And The End Of History*, 1991, Harper San Francisco.

We have much to learn. The stars have not yet written our names in light. Television must die. Vision must be reinvented. Open your eyes to the reality of things: life is an epic commodity with which to illuminate the mind. We want to reach higher ground and live in rarefied air.

You may think you are looked at as suspect, but oftentimes others are aware of your powers before even you. The most difficult period of doubt will come just before you learn to trust your instincts, because in the realm of individual experience the community is not present to witness or explain events outside its collective experience. Trust yourself and your vision. Don't bend your thinking to the thinking of the group. The universe revolves in a spiral around the individual who records his or her experiences for later transmission into the group's pool of things seen, heard, felt, experienced, and understood.

Once our eyes are opened they do not close. The imagination is where we separate ourselves from that which exists so that we may invent that which does not.

Far from being puppets, we are puppet masters. We must reverse the tides of input and consumption. We must be producers of electrical experiences, not just conductors. There is infinity inside infinity. The shaman charges it with life and fills the world with electricity. He or she is life. He or she is light.

Greg Bachar earned his M.F.A. in Creative Writing (Fiction) from the University of Massachusetts, Amherst. He is the author of *CURIOSISOSITY*, *Dumb Bell & Sticky Foot (& Other Indulgences)*, *Beans (& Other Sundry Items From The General Store)*, *Sensual Eye (The Jack Waste Papers Volume I, 1991-2004)*, *Three-Sided Coin (Published Works 1990-2003)*, and *The Writing Machine (Writings About Writing: Occasional Ruminations On An Intangible Legerdemain)*.

Book#2 of 'BEAUTIFULLY UGLY PEOPLE' SERIES

I AM THE
SECRET

Michael D. Beckford

A Michael Beckford Group LLC Subsidiary.

I AM THE SECRET

Isbn-10: 0-9824189-2-2
Isbn-13: 978-0-9824189-2-5

Attention: Schools, Corporations and Non-Profit Businesses

SPEAKPUBLISHING books are available at
quantity discounts with bulk purchase for
educational, business, churches or sales
promotional use. For information please
send an email to speakpubone@gmail.com
With subject: bulk ordering.
Cover design by Michael D. Beckford
Cover Art by Darell Threeths
Typing by Tracy Leggett
Editing by Shantae Charles
www.shantaecharles.com

Third Edition December 2020

Published Digitally and Printed in
the United States of America.